# Teaching A' ' ''---'---

## THE UNIVERSITY OF CHICAGO SCHOOL MATHEMATICS PROJECT

# ALGEBRA

## INTEGRATED MATHEMATICS

Includes Teacher's-Edition
Warm-ups, visual organizers, grids,
charts, graphs, and examples

ISBN: 0-673-45771-0

6–HR–00999897

**Scott Foresman**
**Addison Wesley**

Editorial Offices: Glenview, Illinois • Menlo Park, California
Sales Offices: Reading, Massachusetts • Atlanta, Georgia
Glenview, Illinois • Carrollton, Texas • Menlo Park, California

http://www.sf.aw.com

# Contents

*References in parentheses indicate the first lesson for which the Teaching Aid may be used.

# Warm-up

For 1–4, fill in the blank to make the sentence true.

**1.** A mile is longer than a _____.

**2.** A triangle has _____ sides.

**3.** _____ plays basketball.

**4.** A _____ has four legs.

**5.** Make up a sentence with only one correct response.

# Warm-up

Describe each set of numbers. The three dots mean that the pattern continues.

**1.** {1, 3, 5, 7, 9, . . . }          **2.** {1, 3, 5, 7, 9}

**3.** {0, 1, 4, 9, 16, 25, . . . }     **4.** {2, 3, 5, 7, 11, . . . }

**5.** { . . ., -3, -2, -1, 0, 1, 2, 3, . . . }

# Warm-up

Let $A$ = the set of people whose first and last names begin with a vowel and $B$ = the set of people whose first or last name begins with a vowel.

**1.** Name at least one person in each set. If you cannot think of anyone, make up a name.

**2.** Which set do you think will have more members. Why?

# Warm-up

Put +, −, ×, or ÷ in the blanks below. You do not have to use every symbol, and you may not use any symbol more than once. Following the order of operations, what is the smallest number you can make?

8 _____ 1 _____ 6 _____ 4

# Warm-up

Write a formula that you remember learning at another time. Explain in writing what the formula is about and give an example of its use.

# Warm-up

**1.** Find the area of a square with sides 5 cm long.

**2.** Find the length of a side of a square whose area is 36 cm$^2$.

**3.** Find the area of a square with sides $\sqrt{11}$ cm long.

**4.** Find the length of a side of a square whose area is 7 cm$^2$.

# Warm-up

Give the next three numbers. Then describe the pattern.

**1.** 2, 4, 6, 8, . . .     **2.** -9, -6, -3, 0, 3, . . .

**3.** 5, 9, 13, 17, . . .     **4.** 2, 3, 5, 9, 17, 33, . . .

**5.** 0, 1, 8, 27, 64, . . .

# Warm-up

Work in groups. Use a pen to mark a length of string into 12 equal segments. Then devise a way to use the string to form a right angle. Explain what you did.

# Warm-up

At a back-to-school sale, pens were on sale for 59¢ each and folders were on sale for 19¢ each. For each of the following groups, find the total cost of buying one pen and one folder for every person in the group.

**1.** The girls in your math class

**2.** The boys in your math class

**3.** The students in your grade

**4.** The students in your school

# Real Numbers

**Real Numbers**

**Irrational Numbers**

(infinite non-repeating decimals)

Samples: $\pi$, $\sqrt{2}$, $\sqrt{4.5\overline{3}}$

**Rational Numbers**

(terminating or repeating decimals)

Samples: $\frac{2}{5}$, $-\frac{4}{3}$, 3.56, $-4.\overline{3}$

**Integers**

{. . ., -3, -2, -1, 0, 1, 2, 3, . . .}

Samples: -561, 0, $\frac{12}{3}$, 1 million, $1 \times 10^9$

**Whole Numbers**

{0, 1, 2, 3, . . .}

Samples: 0, one, 2, $\frac{15}{3}$, $\sqrt{25}$

# Number Lines

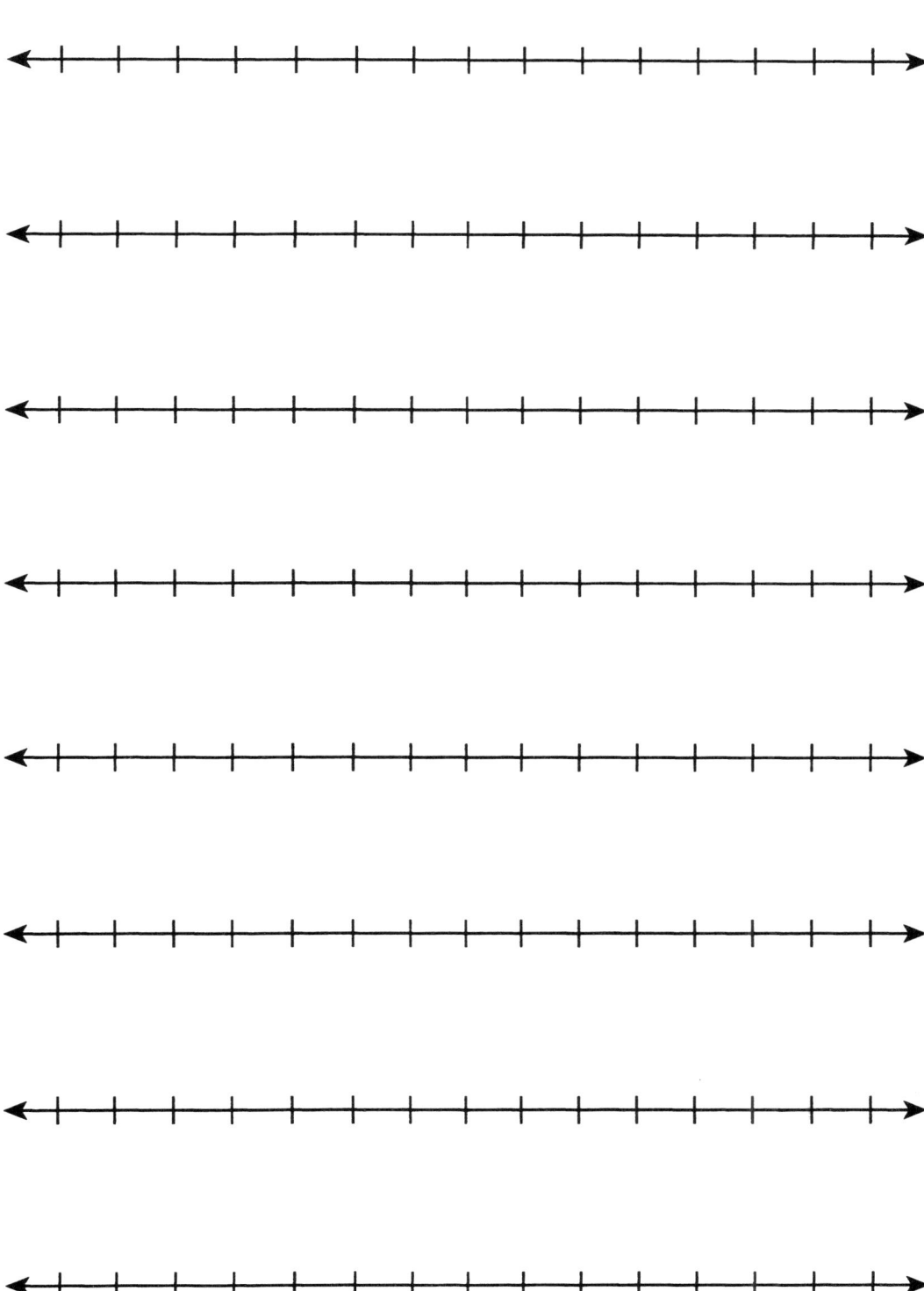

# Number-Line Jeopardy

**1.**

**2.**

**3.**

**4.**

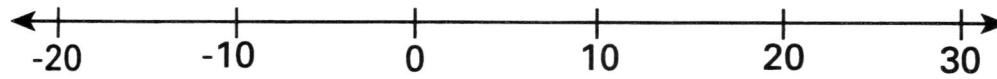

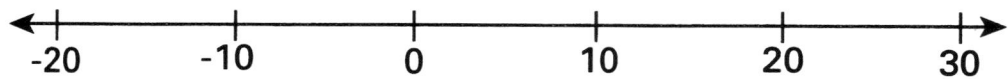

# Squares and Square Roots

| $\sqrt{n}$ | $n$ | $n^2$ |
|---|---|---|
| 1 | 1 | 1 |
| 1.414 | 2 | 4 |
| 1.732 | 3 | 9 |
| 2 | 4 | 16 |
| 2.236 | 5 | 25 |
| 2.449 | 6 | 36 |
| 2.646 | 7 | 49 |
| 2.828 | 8 | 64 |
| 3 | 9 | 81 |
| 3.162 | 10 | 100 |
|  | 11 |  |
|  | 12 |  |
|  | 13 |  |
|  | 14 |  |
|  | 15 |  |
|  | 16 |  |
|  | 17 |  |
|  | 18 |  |
|  | 19 |  |
|  | 20 |  |

# Question 30

| Sun | Mon | Tue | Wed | Thu | Fri | Sat |
|-----|-----|-----|-----|-----|-----|-----|
|     |     |     |     | 1   | 2   | 3   |
| 4   | 5   | 6   | 7   | 8   | 9   | 10  |
| 11  | 12  | 13  | 14  | 15  | 16  | 17  |
| 18  | 19  | 20  | 21  | 22  | 23  | 24  |
| 25  | 26  | 27  | 28  | 29  | 30  | 31  |

_____   _____   _____

_____   $N$   _____

_____   $N + 7$   _____

# Pythagorean Patterns

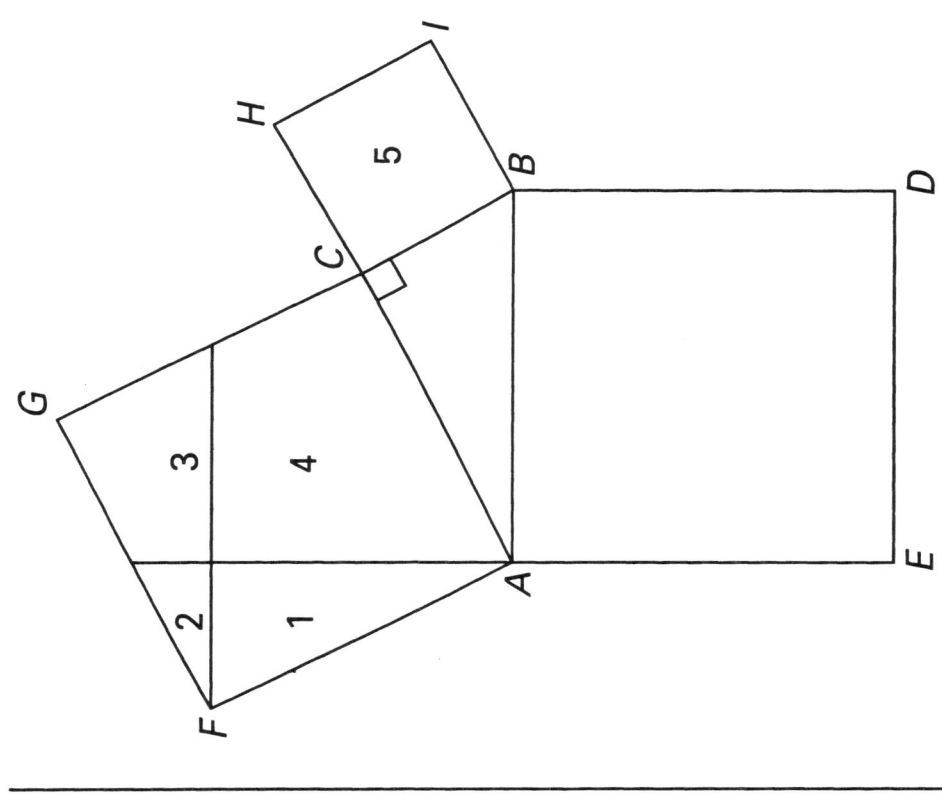

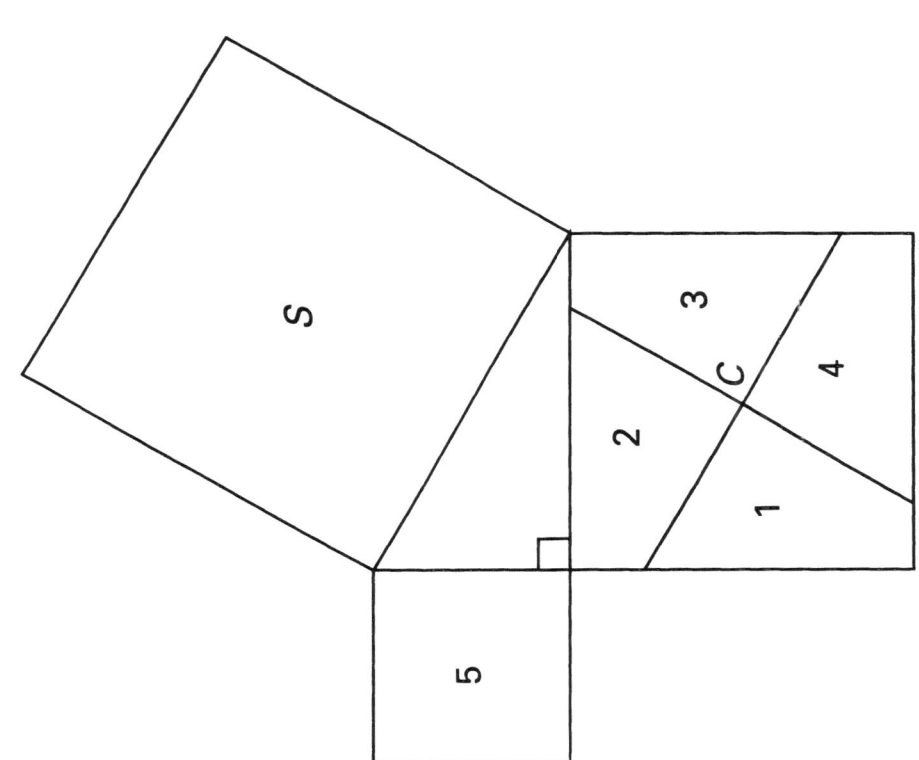

# Question 26

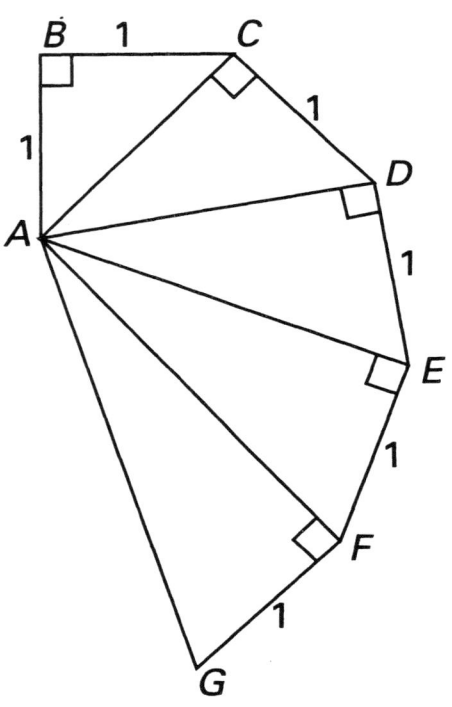

# Additional Examples

**1.** What is the length of the hypotenuse of the right triangle shown at the right?

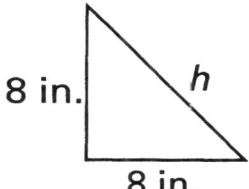

8 in.

8 in.

$h$

**2.** To get to school, Eddie travels 2.5 miles east and 1.5 miles north. If he could travel to school in a straight line, how far would he have to go?

**3.** Central Park in New York City is shaped like a rectangle. It is 0.8 kilometers wide and 4 kilometers long. About how far is it from the southeast corner of the park to the northwest corner?

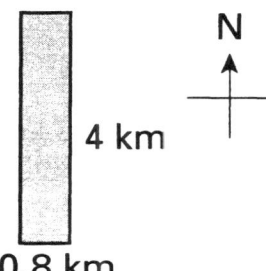

N

4 km

0.8 km

- - - - - - - - - - - - - - - - - - - - - - - - - - - - - - - - - - - - - - - - - - -

# Extension

Show that both squares have sides of length $a + b$. Then work in groups and show that $a^2 + b^2 = c^2$.

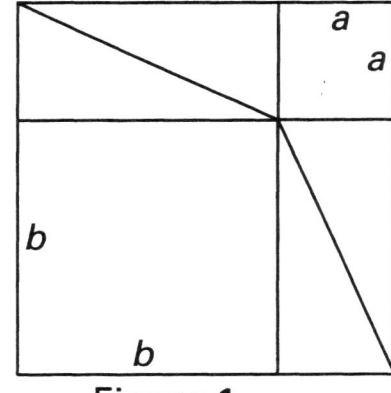

Figure 1

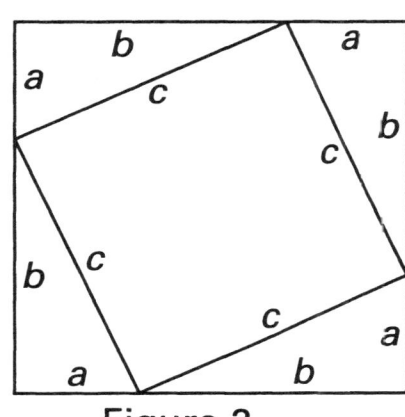

Figure 2

# Centimeter Grid

# Warm-up

Work in groups. Assign numbers to letters of the alphabet, letting $A = 1$, $B = 2$, $C = 3$, and so on.

1. Find the product and the sum of the values of the letters in your first name.

2. Which has the greater value for your name, the product or the sum? Is this relationship true for each name in your group?

3. Which name in your group has the greatest product? the least product?

4. If two people in your group compare their sums and products, does the name with the greater sum always have the greater product?

# Warm-up

1. One cup = _____ pint, so _____ cups = 1 pint.
2. One cup = _____ quart, so _____ cups = 1 quart.
3. One cup = _____ gallon, so _____ cups = 1 gallon.
4. One zaph = $\frac{1}{8}$ zing, so _____ zaphs = 1 zing.
5. One ding = 4 pings, so _____ ding = 1 ping.

# Warm-up

All of the edges of Box A are 12 centimeters long. Box B has half the length, half the width, and one third the height of Box A.

1. What is the volume of Box B?

2. How do the volumes of the two boxes compare?

## Warm-up

Work in groups. Circle all of the rates you can find in the newspaper your teacher gives you. Make a list of the different units in the rates that you have found.

## Warm-up

Evaluate each expression.

**1.** $(-1)^{100}$      **2.** $(-1)^{99}$      **3.** $(-3)^3$

**4.** $-3^3$      **5.** $-3^2$      **6.** $(-3)^2$

## Warm-up

*Multiple choice.* For 1–5, tell which answer is the solution to the equation.

**1.** $13x = 52$    **a.** $x = \frac{1}{4}$    **b.** $x = -4$    **c.** $x = 4$

**2.** $-4.5y = 36$    **a.** $y = 8$    **b.** $y = -8$    **c.** $y = \frac{4}{5}$

**3.** $-6 = -\frac{5}{3}z$    **a.** $z = -\frac{18}{5}$    **b.** $z = 3\frac{1}{5}$    **c.** $z = 3\frac{3}{5}$

**4.** $\frac{-5n}{8} = 1$    **a.** $n = \frac{8}{5}$    **b.** $n = 8$    **c.** $n = -\frac{8}{5}$

**5.** $5 = -5m$    **a.** $m = -\frac{1}{5}$    **b.** $m = -1$    **c.** $m = 0$

## Warm-up

**1.** The reciprocal of -8 is _____.

**2.** The product of 0 and any number is _____.

**3.** The only number without a reciprocal is _____.

**4.** There are two numbers that equal their own reciprocal. They are _____ and _____.

# Warm-up

Give three numbers that make each sentence true.

**1.** $x > -3 + 6$      **2.** $y \geq 0.5 \times 0$      **3.** $z \leq -3 \times -7$

**4.** $m > -4^2$      **5.** $-3 > r > -18$      **6.** $6 < n < 25$

# Warm-up

Answer *true* or *false* for 1–4. You may have to guess.

**1.** The unit of money in Mauritius is the rupee.

**2.** The Prime Minister of Canada in 1900 was Laurier.

**3.** Stan Jok played baseball for the Boston Red Sox.

**4.** Hannah Van Buren's maiden name was Hoes.

**5.** List all the possible ways to answer the four questions. How many possibilities are there?

# Warm-up

Do as many of the following computations as you can without a calculator. Then use a calculator to find the rest of the values.

**1.** $1 \cdot 2 \cdot 3 \cdot 4$

**2.** $1 \cdot 2 \cdot 3 \cdot 4 \cdot 5$

**3.** $1 \cdot 2 \cdot 3 \cdot 4 \cdot 5 \cdot 6$

**4.** $1 \cdot 2 \cdot 3 \cdot 4 \cdot 5 \cdot 6 \cdot 7$

**5.** $1 \cdot 2 \cdot 3 \cdot 4 \cdot 5 \cdot 6 \cdot 7 \cdot 8$

**6.** $1 \cdot 2 \cdot 3 \cdot 4 \cdot 5 \cdot 6 \cdot 7 \cdot 8 \cdot 9$

**7.** $1 \cdot 2 \cdot 3 \cdot 4 \cdot 5 \cdot 6 \cdot 7 \cdot 8 \cdot 9 \cdot 10$

**8.** $\dfrac{1 \cdot 2 \cdot 3 \cdot 4 \cdot 5 \cdot 6 \cdot 7 \cdot 8 \cdot 9}{1 \cdot 2 \cdot 3 \cdot 4 \cdot 5 \cdot 6 \cdot 7}$

# Additional Examples

**1.** Find the area of this figure. All of the angles are right angles. Explain how you found the area.

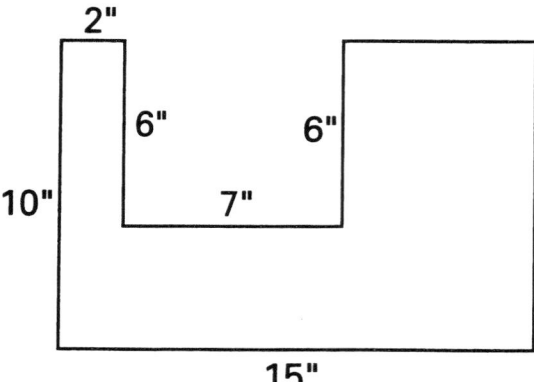

**2.** The Stuart Soup Company packs soup cans in cartons that are 40 cm wide, 48 cm long, and 20 cm tall. Find the volume of the carton.

**3.** If a box has dimensions $\ell = \frac{5}{2}$ in., $w = \frac{1}{2}$ in., and $h = 6$ in., find the volume using the formulas below.

**a.** $V = \ell wh$     **b.** $V = Bh$

**4.** What is the area of this figure? All of the angles are right angles.

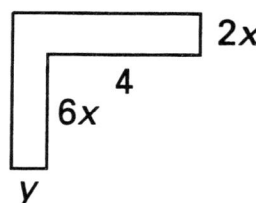

# Dot Paper

# Additional Examples

1. It takes Felicia 25 minutes to walk one mile. At this rate, how long would it take her to walk 7 miles?

2. If a car travels 55 miles an hour, about how far will it travel in $3\frac{3}{4}$ hours?

3. If a car travels at 55 miles an hour, how far does it travel per second?

4. Refer to Example 4 on page 93. An average-sized person burns about 500 calories per hour swimming. If a person swims for a half hour, how much weight will he or she lose?

5. Suppose gasoline costs $1.20 a gallon. State the reciprocal rate and explain how it describes the same situation.

6. In 1962, Wilt Chamberlain set an NBA season scoring record, averaging 50.4 points per game. On the average, how many points did he score per minute? (There are 48 minutes in a basketball game.)

# Balance-Scale Diagrams

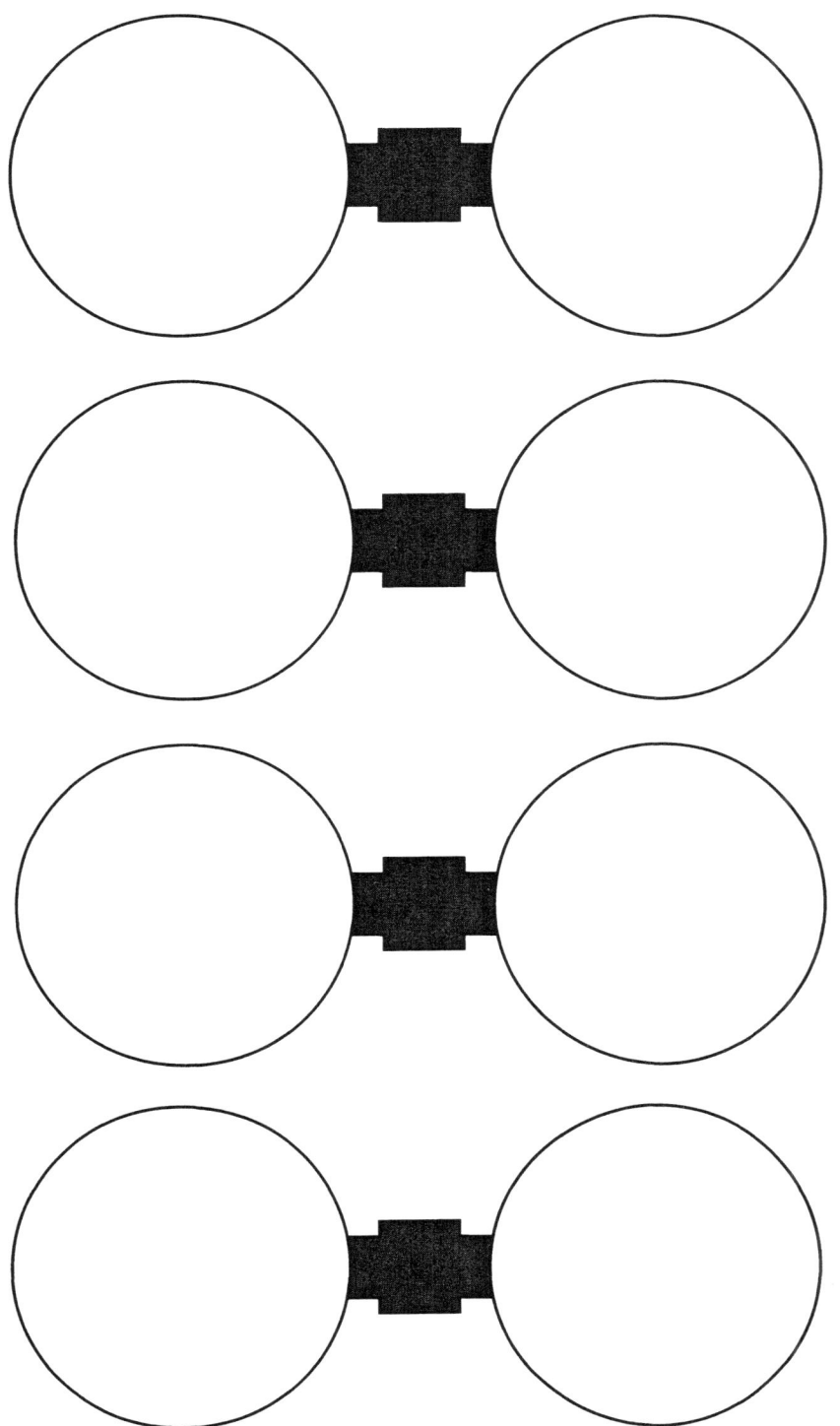

# Additional Examples 2-5

**2.** A restaurant offers a special breakfast of eggs, meat, and juice. The eggs can be cooked in one of three different ways (scrambled, fried, poached); there are two choices for the meat (bacon, sausage) and three choices for the juice (orange, grapefruit, tomato). How many different breakfasts can be ordered?

**3.** While Kari was at summer camp, it was sunny for 7 days, and then it rained for 3 days. Each day Kari could do one special activity. On sunny days she had her choice of five different outside activities, and on rainy days she had her choice of two different inside activities. In how many ways could she choose her special activities?

**4. a.** A test has 10 true-false items and 15 multiple-choice items with 4 choices each. How many different answer sheets are possible?

  **b.** A test has $T$ true-false items and $M$ multiple-choice items with 4 choices each. How many different answer sheets are possible?

**5.** Suppose Mrs. Smith writes a chapter test that has 12 questions. It has four multiple-choice questions, each with $r$ possible answers, three multiple-choice questions, each with $p$ possible answers, and five true-false questions. How many ways are there to answer the questions?

# Warm-up

Use the information on page 141. Plan a breakfast by estimating what you think are reasonable quantities of orange juice, corn flakes, scrambled eggs, toast, and whole milk.

**1.** How many calories are in your breakfast?

**2.** Write the formula for the total amount of protein in your breakfast.

**3.** How many grams of protein are in your breakfast?

# Warm-up

Explain how to determine the sign of a sum of two numbers.

# Warm-up

Suppose that your school is at the origin.

**1.** Show the location of your home on the graph. Describe the location in terms of a distance (miles) east or west of the school and a distance north or south of the school.

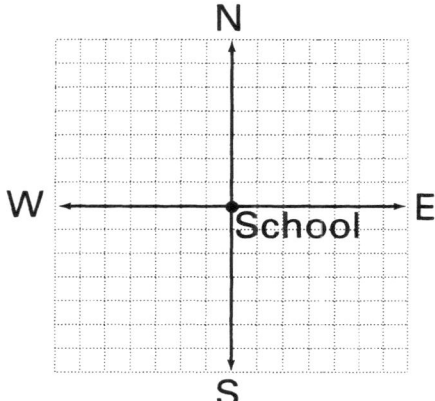

**2.** Show two other locations on the graph, and describe each of them.

# Warm-up

Name four points that are 1 unit away from (98, 32).

# Warm-up

Write the opposite and the reciprocal of each number.

**1.** -9     **2.** $\frac{2}{3}$     **3.** 12     **4.** 1.5     **5.** -20

**6.** $\frac{1}{8}$     **7.** -4     **8.** 16     **9.** $-2\frac{1}{2}$     **10.** 3.65

# Warm-up

A pack of NBA basketball cards costs $2.19. Ellen bought four packs of cards last week, three packs yesterday, and two packs today.

**1.** How much did she spend on basketball cards, excluding tax?

**2.** Explain two ways in which you can find the answer.

# Warm-up

Simplify each expression.

**1.** $2x^2 + x^2 + 5$       **2.** $y^2 + y + 4y + 2$

**3.** $6 + z^2 + -z^2 + 1$       **4.** $4a + -3a + 8a$

**5.** $b^2 + 7b + 2 + 6b + -2$       **6.** $-6 + 7 + 4 + -2 + 3 + 2$

# Warm-up
**Lesson 3-8**

Students collected food for a food drive and displayed canned goods in a pyramid. The top three rows of the pyramid are shown at the right.

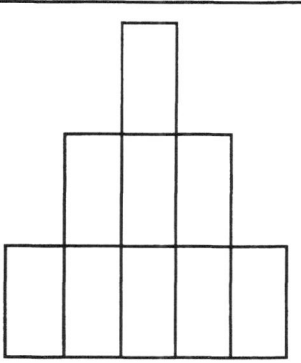

How many cans are in the

**1.** fourth row?

**2.** sixth row?

**3.** tenth row?

# Warm-up
**Lesson 3-9**

Write a letter to a student who has not studied algebra, explaining in your own words how to add fractions with different denominators.

# Warm-up
**Lesson 3-10**

Tell whether -3 is a solution to the sentence.

**1.** $-3n + -9 \geq 0$

**2.** $\dfrac{4m}{m + 1} \leq -6$

**3.** $2p + 1 > 1$

**4.** $-\dfrac{x}{x} = 1$

**5.** $y - 3 < 0$

**6.** $-5z + 2z = -9$

# Additional Examples

**1.** Paula baby-sat on three days last week: 2 hours on Monday, *w* hours on Wednesday, and $3\frac{1}{2}$ hours on Saturday. Altogether, she baby-sat for 8 hours. Write an equation relating *w* and the other quantities.

**2.** During a drought, the level of Cottonwood Creek dropped 18 inches. After a storm, it rose 2 inches. Later, the level dropped 4 inches.
   **a.** Find the net change.
   **b.** As a check, picture this situation on a number line.

**3.** Ms. Worth was driving at 40 miles per hour. She sped up 15 miles an hour and then slowed down 20 miles an hour. Write an addition problem to represent these changes, and find her resulting speed.

**4.** Simplify $(-6 + j) + (15 + k)$.

**5.** Mr. Carlson is making a set of shelves. He started with a board *t* feet long. He cut off 3 shelves, each of which is 2 feet long, and he has a piece *e* feet long left over. Write a formula for *t* in terms of e.

# Addition and Multiplication Properties

|  | Addition | Multiplication |
|---|---|---|
| Identity Property | $a + 0 = a$ | $a \cdot 1 = a$ |
| Inverse Property | $a + \text{-}a = 0$ | For $a \neq 0$, $a \cdot \dfrac{1}{a} = 1$ |
| Commutative Property | $a + b = b + a$ | $a \cdot b = b \cdot a$ |
| Associative Property | $a + (b + c) = (a + b) + c$ | $a \cdot (b \cdot c) = (a \cdot b) \cdot c$ |

-------------------------------------------------------------

# Challenge

The operation ♣ is defined below over the set $S = \{a, b, c, t\}$.

| ♣ | a | b | c | t |
|---|---|---|---|---|
| a | b | t | a | t |
| b | t | c | b | a |
| c | a | b | c | t |
| t | t | a | t | b |

**1.** Does this operation have an identity element? If so, what is it?

**2.** Is this operation commutative? If no, give a counterexample.

**3.** Is this operation associative? If no, give a counterexample.

# Graph Paper

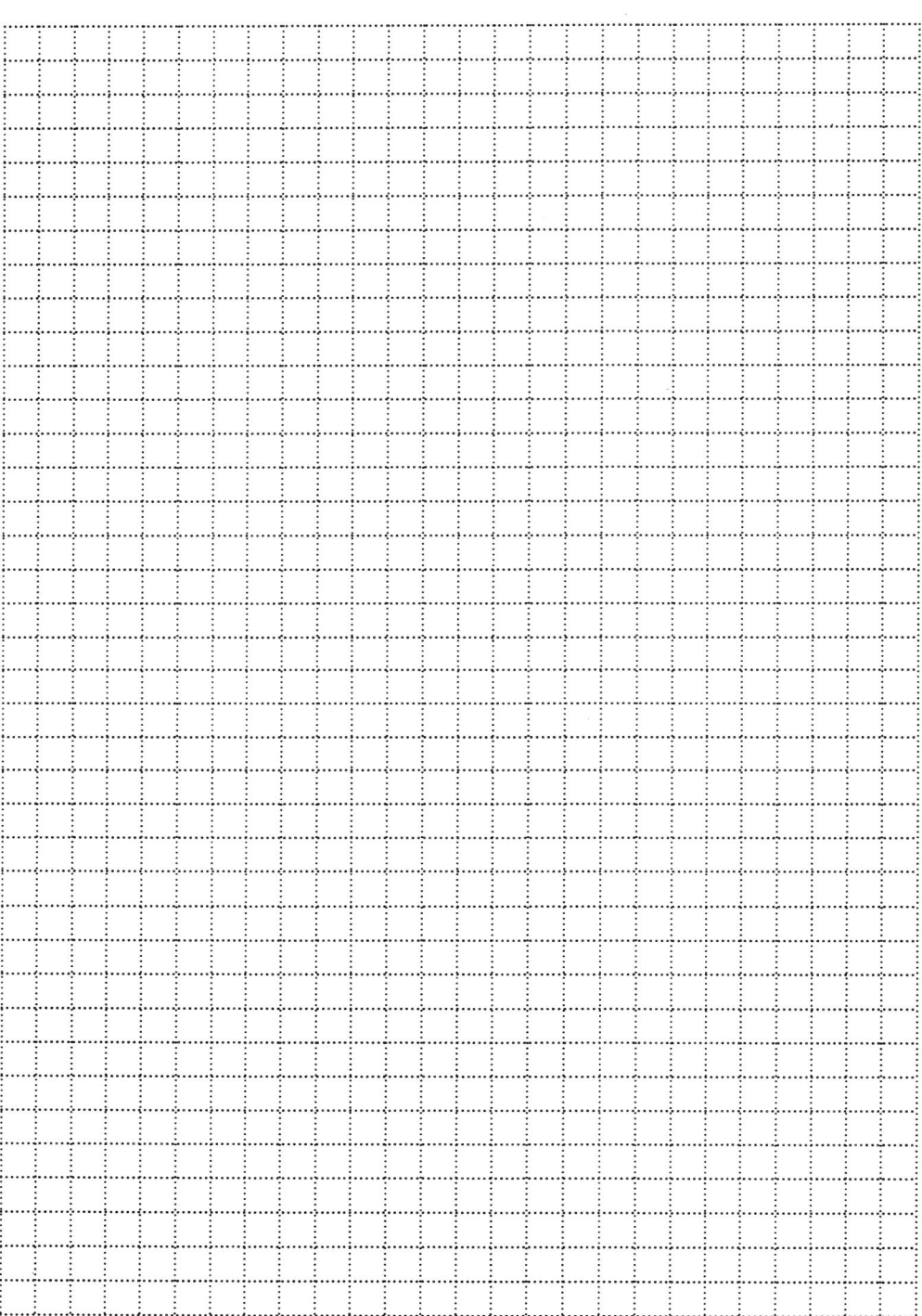

# Additional Examples 2, 4 and 5

**2.** The average normal monthly temperatures (Fahrenheit) in Barrow, Alaska, are:

| | | | |
|---|---|---|---|
| Jan. -14° | Feb. -20° | Mar. -16° | Apr. -2° |
| May 19° | June 33° | July 39° | Aug. 38° |
| Sept. 31° | Oct. 14° | Nov. -1° | Dec. -13° |

  **a.** Graph the temperatures.
  **b.** When is the average temperature above freezing?
  **c.** Describe the temperature changes.

**4.** The graph shows the number of people who were in a classroom over a period of time. Write a story that explains the graph.

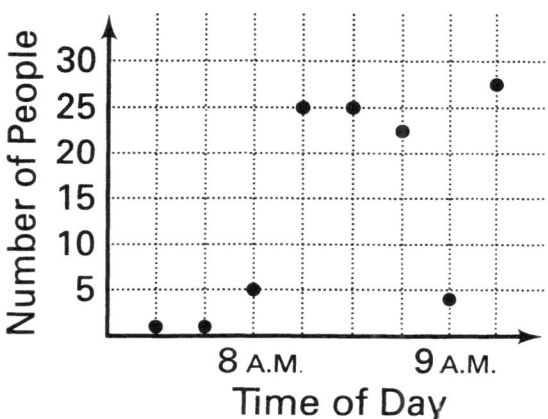

**5.** A graph can be made purposely misleading. The two graphs show the same data. Which graph is misleading and why?

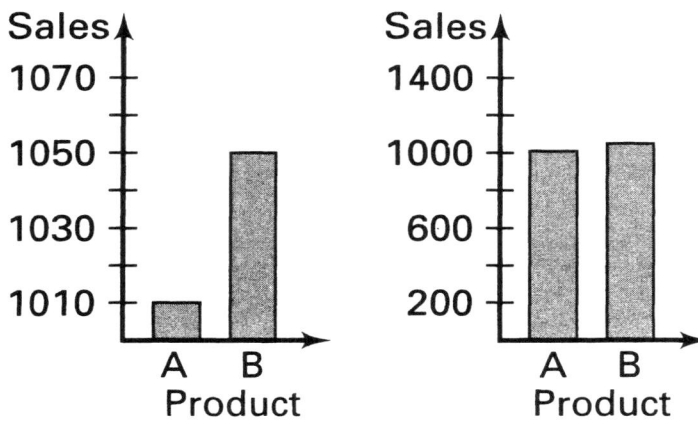

# Four-Quadrant Graph Paper

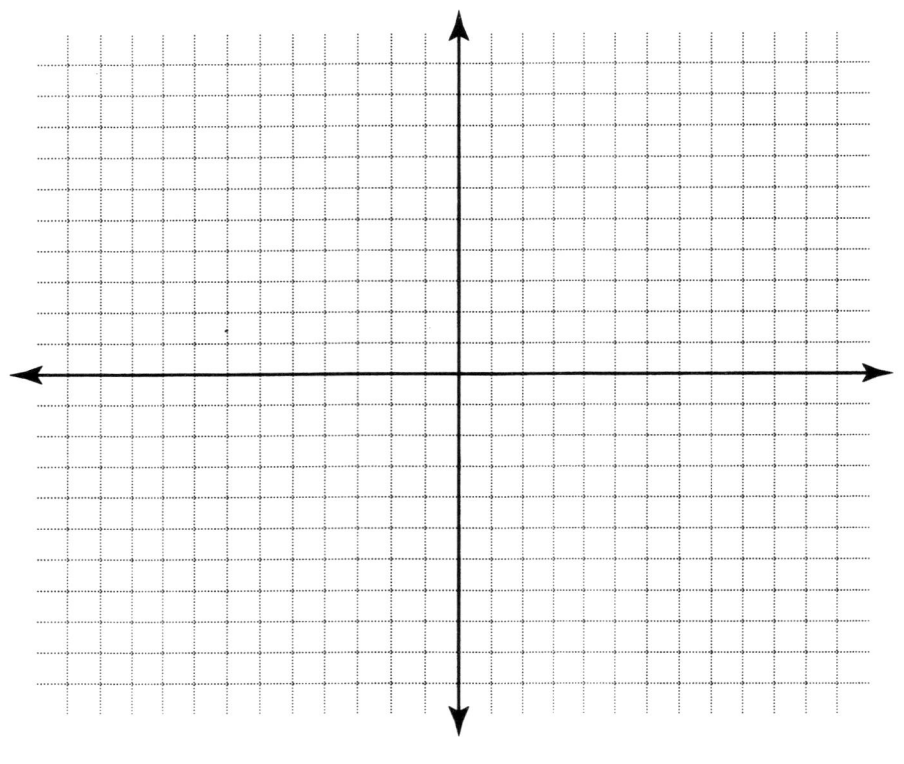

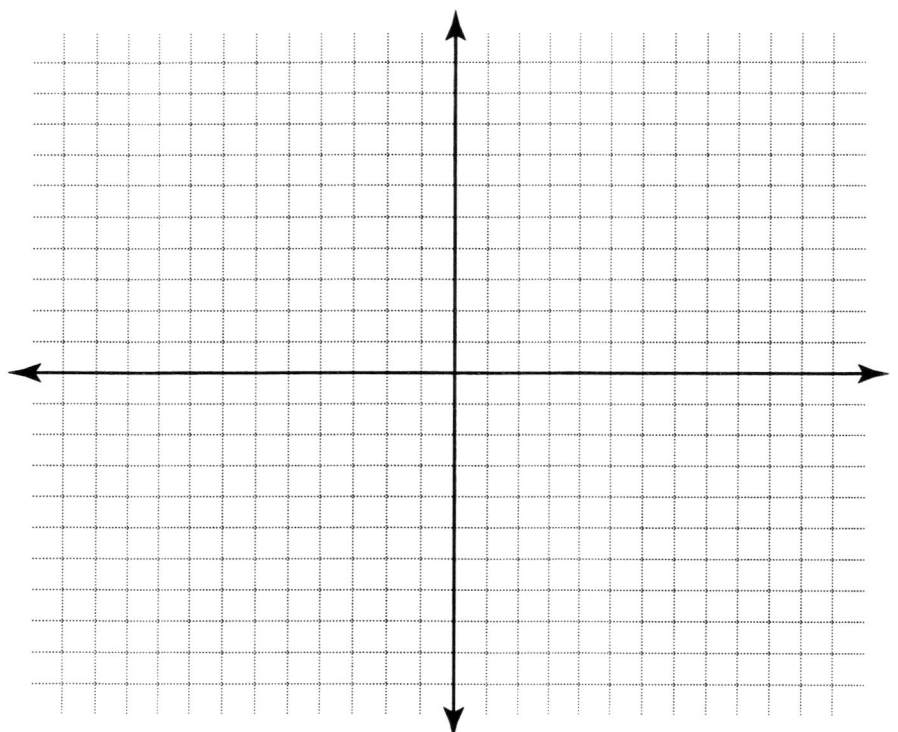

# Examples 1 and 2

## Example 1

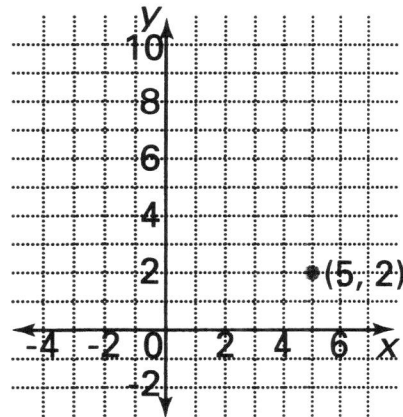

## Example 2

# Activity

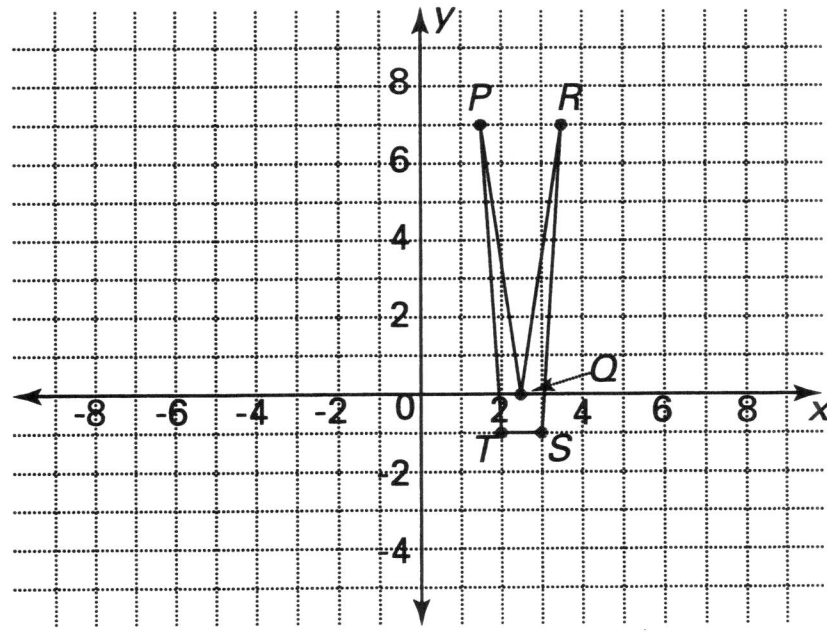

# Additional Examples

**1. a.** Plot $\triangle RTX$, where $R = (-4, -1)$, $T = (3, 1)$ and $X = (0, -4)$.
   **b.** Draw the image $R'T'X'$ after sliding left 3 units and up 7 units. Find the coordinates of $R'$, $T'$, and $X'$.

**2.** Give the coordinates of the image of $(x, y)$ under a slide 4 units to the left.

**3.** The ears of a rabbit are shown in the Activity on page 165. On the graph below, Figure $STUVW$ shows the head of the rabbit. Use the rule that the image of $(x, y)$ is $(x + -5, y + 2)$, and draw the image of this figure. Label the image $S'T'U'V'W'$.

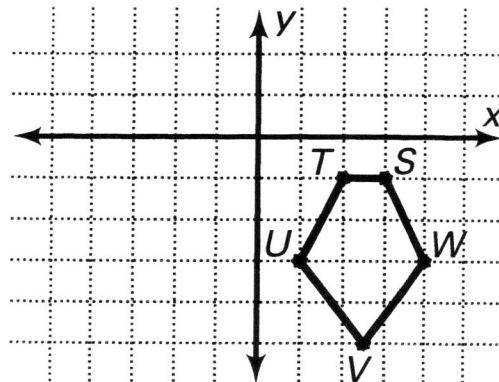

**4.** Find the images of points $P = (7, 2)$ and $Q = (-8, 1)$ under a slide of 6 units to the right and 5 units down.

# Algebra Tiles

| $x^2$ | $x$ | $x$ | $x$ | $x$ | $x$ |
|-------|-----|-----|-----|-----|-----|
| $x^2$ | $x$ | $x$ | $x$ | $x$ | $x$ |
| $x^2$ | 1 | 1 | 1 | 1 | 1 |
|       | 1 | 1 | 1 | 1 | 1 |
|       | 1 | 1 | 1 | 1 | 1 |
|       | 1 | 1 | 1 | 1 | 1 |

# Additional Examples 1–4

Use the pattern below for 1–3.

1st            2nd            3rd

**1.** Suppose each succeeding design is made by adding 7 stars to the previous design. How many stars will the 4th design in the pattern contain?

**2.** How many stars are needed for the
    **a.** 8th design?     **b.** $n$th design?

**3.** If a design is made with 80 stars, what design number in the sequence is it?

**4.** If it costs $1.50 for the first hour and $0.60 for each additional hour to park in a large city, what does it cost to park for $n$ hours?

---

# Challenge

Find the perimeter of diagrams that have 1, 2, 3, 4 and 5 pentagons. Then write an expression for the perimeter of a diagram with $n$ pentagons.

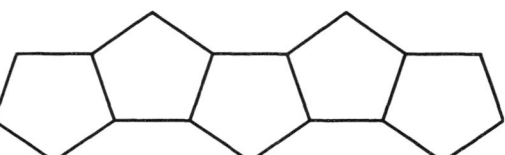

# Warm-up

Simplify.

**1.** $r - 2s + 5r + -2s$

**2.** $\frac{1}{2}m + \frac{3}{4}n - \frac{2}{3}m - 2\frac{3}{4}n$

**3.** $.3p - q - p - 3q$

Evaluate both the original expression and your simplified answer to Questions 1, 2, and 3 when

**4.** $r = 2$ and $s = 3$.

**5.** $m = 12$ and $n = 4$.

**6.** $p = 5$ and $q = 2$.

# Warm-up

Use the figure to answer the questions. *ABCD* and *ARST* are both squares.

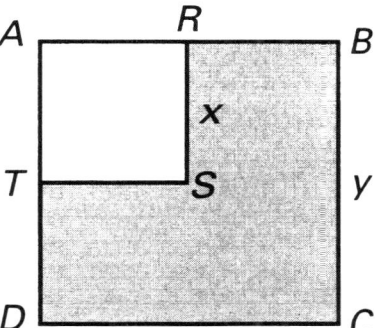

**1.** What information is necessary to determine the area of the shaded region?

**2.** What is the area of the shaded region in terms of *x* and *y*?

**3.** Find the area of the shaded region if $x = 2.7$ cm and $y = 7$ cm.

# Warm-up

Find the difference between the record high and low temperatures for each of these states.

**1.** Alaska:  High: 100°F (June 27, 1915)
      Low:  -80°F (January 23, 1971)

**2.** Florida: High: 109°F (June 29, 1931)
      Low:  -2°F (February 13, 1899)

**3.** Pennsylvania:  High: 111°F (July 10, 1936)
      Low:  -42°F (January 5, 1904)

**4.** Nevada: High:  122°F (June 26, 1990)
      Low:   -50°F (January 8, 1937)

**5.** California:  High: 134°F (July 10, 1913)
      Low:  -45°F (January 20, 1937)

# Warm-up

The following students took three quizzes and received these scores.

Rosa: 83, 88, 84
Al: 83, 86, 92
Sam: 80, 78, 88
Liz: 76, 85, 91

**1.** Compute each student's average (mean) score.

**2.** Organize the data from Question 1 in a table. Label the columns "Name," "Q 1," "Q 2," "Q 3," and "Avg." Label the rows under "Name" with students' names. Save your table for later use.

# Warm-up

Fill in the table. Select your own values for *a* and *b* in row 5.

|  | *a* | *b* | -(*a* + *b*) | -*a* + -*b* | -*a* – *b* |
|---|---|---|---|---|---|
| **1.** | 2 | 3 |  |  |  |
| **2.** | -2 | 3 |  |  |  |
| **3.** | 2 | -3 |  |  |  |
| **4.** | -2 | -3 |  |  |  |
| **5.** |  |  |  |  |  |

**6.** What do you notice about -(*a* + *b*), -*a* + -*b*, and -*a* – *b*?

# Warm-up

Explain how to plot the ordered pair (*a, b*) on a coordinate graph. Remember that *a* and *b* can be either positive or negative.

# Warm-up

**1.** The sum of the measures of two angles is 90°. The angles are _____ angles.

**2.** A triangle has a 90° angle. It is called a _____ triangle.

**3.** The sum of the angle measures in any triangle is _____.

**4.** The sum of the measures of two angles is 180°. The angles are _____ angles.

## Warm-up

Mr. Smith is going to the hardware store and then to the grocery store. After shopping for groceries, he is going home. He lives 6 miles from the hardware store and 5 miles from the grocery store. Sketch the location of Mr. Smith's home and the two stores for each case.

Case 1: Mr. Smith's trip is as short as possible.
Case 2: Mr. Smith's trip is as long as possible.
Case 3: Mr. Smith's trip is somewhere between the shortest and longest trip.

## Warm-up

For 1–3, tell if the line shows a constant-increase pattern, a constant-decrease pattern, or no increase or decrease.

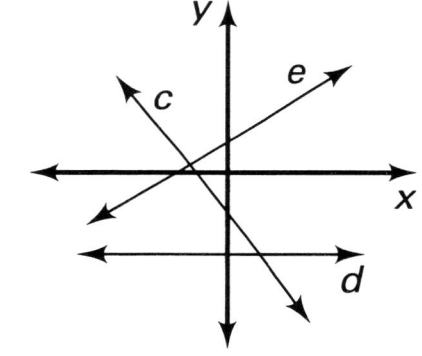

**1.** Line c

**2.** Line d

**3.** Line e

For 4–6, describe the line in words or draw an example of the line on the same grid as lines c, d, and e.

**4.** Line r showing no increase or decrease

**5.** Line s showing a constant decrease

**6.** Line t showing a constant increase

ALGEBRA © Scott, Foresman and Company

# Spreadsheet

|   | A | B | C | D | E | F | G |
|---|---|---|---|---|---|---|---|
| 1 |   |   |   |   |   |   |   |
| 2 |   |   |   |   |   |   |   |
| 3 |   |   |   |   |   |   |   |
| 4 |   |   |   |   |   |   |   |
| 5 |   |   |   |   |   |   |   |
| 6 |   |   |   |   |   |   |   |
| 7 |   |   |   |   |   |   |   |
| 8 |   |   |   |   |   |   |   |
| 9 |   |   |   |   |   |   |   |
| 10 |   |   |   |   |   |   |   |
| 11 |   |   |   |   |   |   |   |
| 12 |   |   |   |   |   |   |   |
| 13 |   |   |   |   |   |   |   |
| 14 |   |   |   |   |   |   |   |
| 15 |   |   |   |   |   |   |   |
| 16 |   |   |   |   |   |   |   |
| 17 |   |   |   |   |   |   |   |
| 18 |   |   |   |   |   |   |   |
| 19 |   |   |   |   |   |   |   |
| 20 |   |   |   |   |   |   |   |
| 21 |   |   |   |   |   |   |   |
| 22 |   |   |   |   |   |   |   |
| 23 |   |   |   |   |   |   |   |
| 24 |   |   |   |   |   |   |   |
| 25 |   |   |   |   |   |   |   |
| 26 |   |   |   |   |   |   |   |
| 27 |   |   |   |   |   |   |   |

# Additional Examples 1 and 2

**1.** The spreadsheet below shows the number of tickets sold and the revenue from ticket sales for a 3-game soccer tournament.

|   | A | B | C | D |
|---|---|---|---|---|
| **1** | Game | | Sales | $$$ |
| **2** | 9 A.M. | | 280 | 700 |
| **3** | 2 P.M. | | 174 | 435 |
| **4** | 7 P.M. | | 321 | |
| **5** | | | | |
| **6** | Total | | | |

**a.** Which cell contains the word "Total"?

**b.** What is in cell C2?

**c.** Which cell contains the number 174?

**d.** Cell C6 is computed by typing "=C2+C3+C4". What number will appear in C6?

**e.** What is in cell D5?

**f.** If the number in C4 is changed to 327, what other entry will change? What will it become?

**2.** Make a spreadsheet to give examples of two ways to find the perimeter of a rectangle: $\ell + w + \ell + w = 2\ell + 2w$.

**a.** Label the columns and rows of your spreadsheet. Fill in row 1.

**b.** Pick values for $\ell$ and $w$. Where will you write them?

**c.** What formula will you write in C2? What will cell C2 show?

**d.** What formula will you write in D2? What will cell D2 show?

# Graphing Equations

Equation: _____

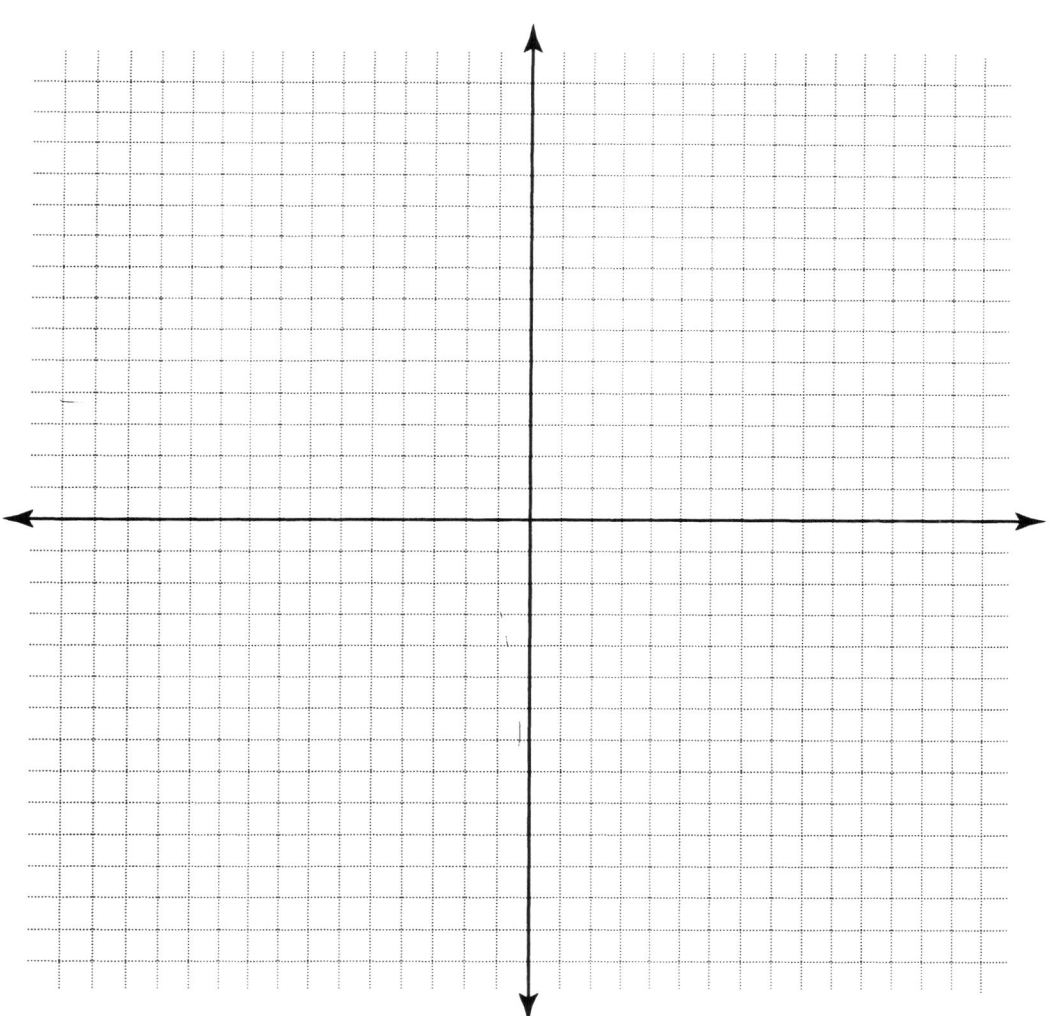

# Question 27

**Party Membership of United States Senators**

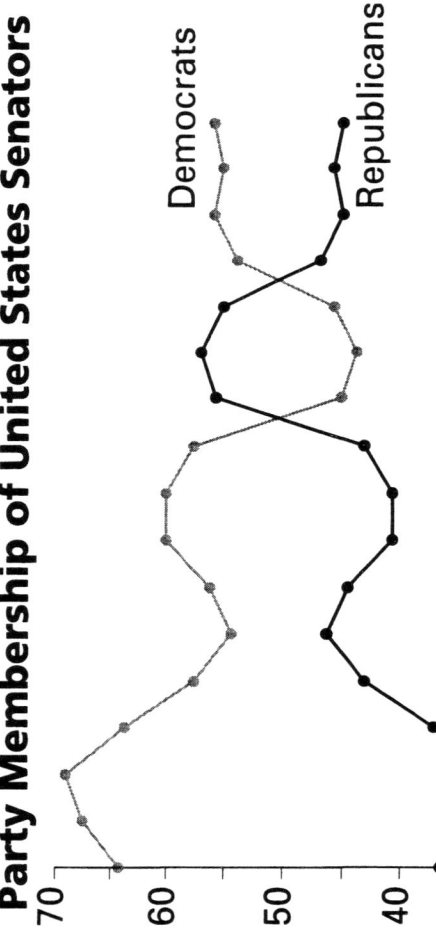

Democrats

Republicans

Number of Senators

70 — 60 — 50 — 40 — 30

61 63 65 67 69 71 73 75 77 79 81 83 85 87 89 91 93
Year

2. How many senators were there for each year represented in the graph?

3. Using your knowledge of government, tell how many senators there are from each state. How many states are there?

4. Under what condition would the graph be perfectly symmetrical?

**1.** Complete the table using the graph.

| Year | 61 | 63 | 65 | 67 | 69 | 71 | 73 | 75 | 77 | 79 | 81 | 83 | 85 | 87 | 89 | 91 | 93 |
|------|----|----|----|----|----|----|----|----|----|----|----|----|----|----|----|----|----|
| No. Rep. | 36 | 33 | 32 | | | | | | | | | | | | | | |
| No. of Dem. | 64 | 67 | 68 | | | | | | | | | | | | | | |
| No. of others | 0 | 0 | 0 | 0 | 0 | 2 | 2 | 2 | 1 | 1 | 1 | 0 | 0 | 0 | 0 | 0 | 0 |
| Total | 100 | 100 | 100 | | | | | | | | | | | | | | |

# Activity

**a.** Measure all the angles in each triangle below, and find the sum of the angle measures.

**b.** Draw another triangle of a different size and shape. Measure its angles and find the sum of its angle measures.

**c.** What patterns do you notice?

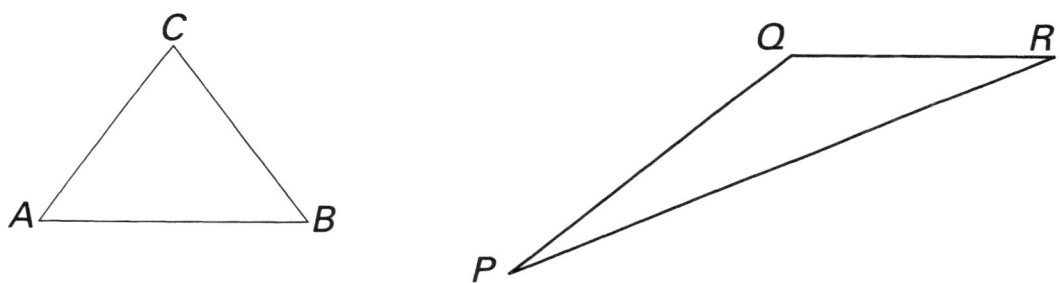

# Question 32

# The Triangle Inequality

| Lengths of Straws | | | Triangle? (Yes or No) | Compare. Use <, >, or =. | | |
|---|---|---|---|---|---|---|
| r | s | t | | $r + s \underline{\ ?\ } t$ | $s + t \underline{\ ?\ } r$ | $r + t \underline{\ ?\ } s$ |
| a. | 1 in. | 2 in. | 2 in. | | | |
| b. | 3 in. | 3 in. | 6 in | | | |
| c. | 3 in. | 6 in. | 1 in. | | | |
| d. | 2 in. | 3 in. | 4 in. | | | |
| e. | 2 in. | 2 in. | 3 in. | | | |
| f. | 5 in. | 2 in. | 3 in. | | | |
| g. | 3 in. | 4 in. | 5 in. | | | |
| h. | 1 in. | 2 in. | 5 in. | | | |

# Example 1

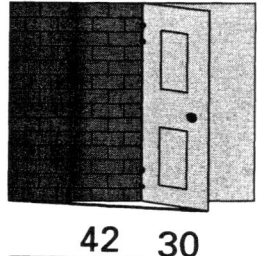
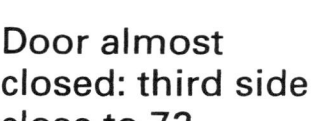

Door almost
closed: third side
close to 72

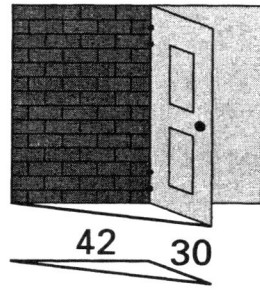

Door partially
open: third side
between 72 and 12

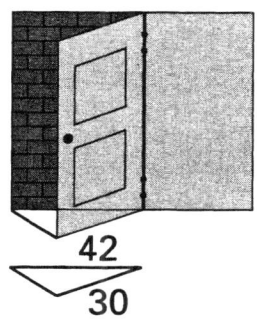

Door almost
flat against
the wall: third
side close to 12

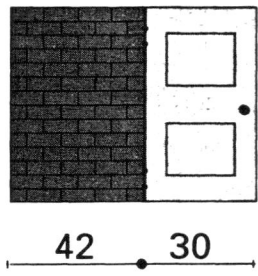

Door closed: no
triangle, distance
42 + 30 = 72

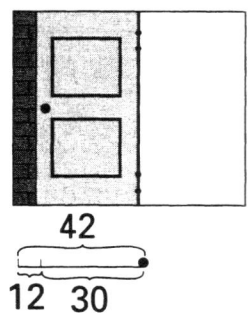

Door completely
open and flat
against the wall:
no triangle,
distance 42 — 30 = 12

# Additional Examples

**1.** If two sides of a triangle have lengths 3 and 19, write an interval to describe the possible lengths of the third side.

**2.** Two sides of a triangle each have length 5 cm. What are the possible lengths of the third side?

|                 | Charlotte | Greensboro | Winston-Salem | Raleigh |
|-----------------|-----------|------------|---------------|---------|
| Charlotte       | ----      | 96         | 81            | 169     |
| Greensboro      | 96        | ----       | 26            | 83      |
| Winston-Salem   | 81        | 26         | ----          | 106     |
| Raleigh         | 169       | 83         | 106           | ----    |

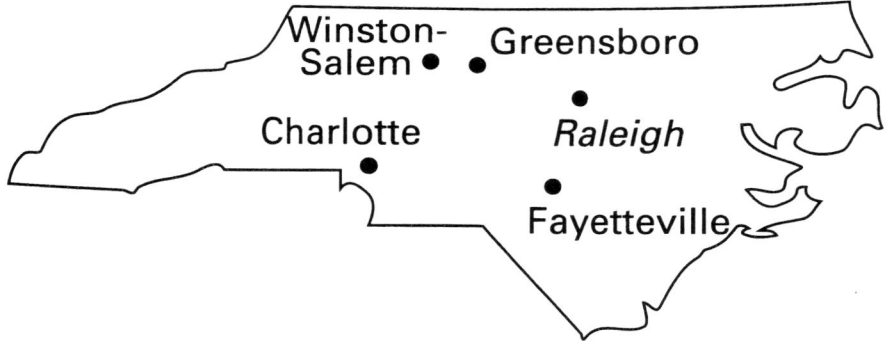

**3. a.** Use the information in the mileage table above to show an example of the Triangle Inequality.
   **b.** It is 66 miles from Raleigh to Fayetteville. From this information, what can you tell about the distance from Charlotte to Fayetteville?

# Question 24

## Years of Life Expected at Birth

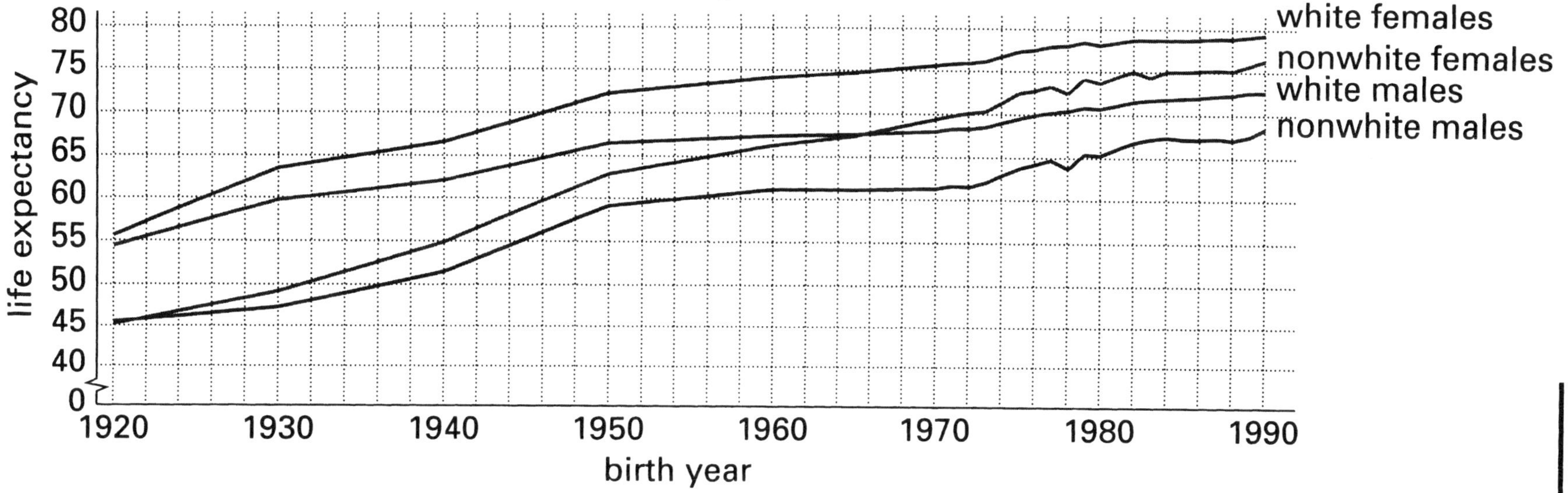

white females
nonwhite females
white males
nonwhite males

life expectancy

80
75
70
65
60
55
50
45
40
0

1920    1930    1940    1950    1960    1970    1980    1990

birth year

# Graphing Constant Increase and Decrease

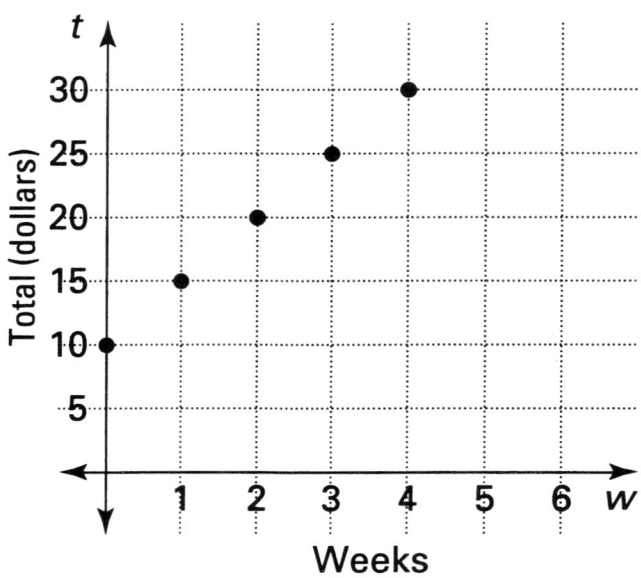

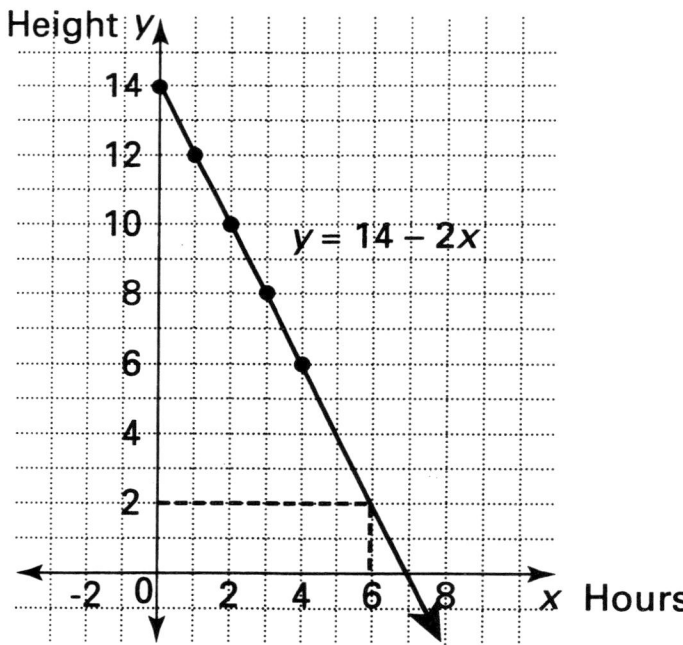

# Warm-up

Work in small groups. Use the information on light bulbs given on page 283.

**1.** Can you tell how much each bulb costs? If so, how much?

**2.** Can you tell how much it costs to operate each bulb? If so, how much?

**3.** Look at the algebraic sentences under the table and graph. What do the numbers represent?

# Warm-up

At Carl's City Car Park, it costs $7.75 to park for 3 hours or less. After 3 hours, it costs $1.25 for each additional hour or fraction of an hour, up to a maximum of $15 for 12 hours.

**1.** Make a table to show the costs of parking for 1 through 12 hours.

**2.** Describe a graph showing this information.

# Warm-up

Decide if each solution is correct. If not, what is the correct solution?

**1.** $x - 16 = 32$; $x = 16$      **2.** $3x + 7 = 11$; $x = 3$

**3.** $-72 - y = -4y$; $y = -24$      **4.** $8 = 0.05n - 2$; $n = 200$

**5.** $23 - n = 5n - 85$; $n = 18$

## Warm-up

Graph the following situations on the same coordinate plane. Then answer the questions by looking at the graphs.

At restaurant A, the salad bar costs $0.25 per ounce. A cup of soup is $0.60 and a beverage costs $0.90.

At restaurant B, the salad bar costs $0.20 per ounce. A cup of soup is $0.75 and a beverage is $1.25.

When is salad, soup, and beverage
**1.** at restaurant A more expensive than at restaurant B?

**2.** at B more expensive than A?

**3.** the same price at both restaurants?

## Warm-up

Solve each equation for $y$.

**1.** $x + y = 8$　　　**2.** $y - 2 = 4x$　　　**3.** $x - y = 9$

**4.** $x - y = -4$　　　**5.** $y + 1 = 7x$

## Warm-up

Write a paragraph explaining how solving $-6x + 3 = 21$ is the same as, and how it is different from, solving $-6x + 3 > 21$. Solve each sentence.

# Warm-up

Laura's parents want to encourage her to save part of the money she earns or receives as gifts. They will add $5 to every deposit each time she deposits half of her money in a bank. The table below shows some instances of this situation.

| $x$ | 100 | 50 | 48 | ? | 20 | 10 |
|---|---|---|---|---|---|---|
| $y$ | 55 | 30 | 29 | 21 | 15 | ? |

**1.** What do $x$ and $y$ represent?

**2.** For what numbers do the question marks stand?

**3.** Write a formula for
   **a.** $y$ in terms of $x$.     **b.** $x$ in terms of $y$.

# Warm-up

Work in groups.

**1.** Study the following equation:
   $48x + 96 = 96x - 480$. Can you solve it quickly?

**2.** What might you do to both sides of the equation to make finding the solution easier?

**3.** Give an equivalent equation that is easier to solve. Then solve it and check your solution in the original equation.

# Warm-up

Work in groups to solve this equation:

$4(3x + 5) + 8(3x + 5) - 2 = 9(3x + 5) + 13$.

# Additional Examples

**1.** Charles received $8 allowance for each of the first five weeks of the year. Imagine that the points (1, 8), (2, 8), (3, 8), (4, 8), and (5, 8) are graphed to represent this situation.

   **a.** What kind of line contains these points, a horizontal line or a vertical line?

   **b.** What is an equation for the line?

**2.** Graph $y = -4$
   **a.** on a number line.    **b.** on a coordinate plane.

**3.** Use the situation described in Example 3 on page 287. Suppose that Mac does not have to pay a service fee when his account is under $300. Explain how to use a graph to find the time at which Mac will have a balance of $100 in his account.

**4. a.** Write an equation for the line containing $(-\frac{1}{2}, 6)$ and $(-\frac{1}{2}, -6)$.

   **b.** Tell whether the line is horizontal, vertical, or neither.

**5.** Give a sentence describing all points on the boundary of the shaded region.

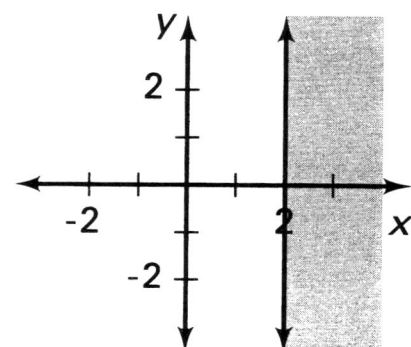

# Question 22

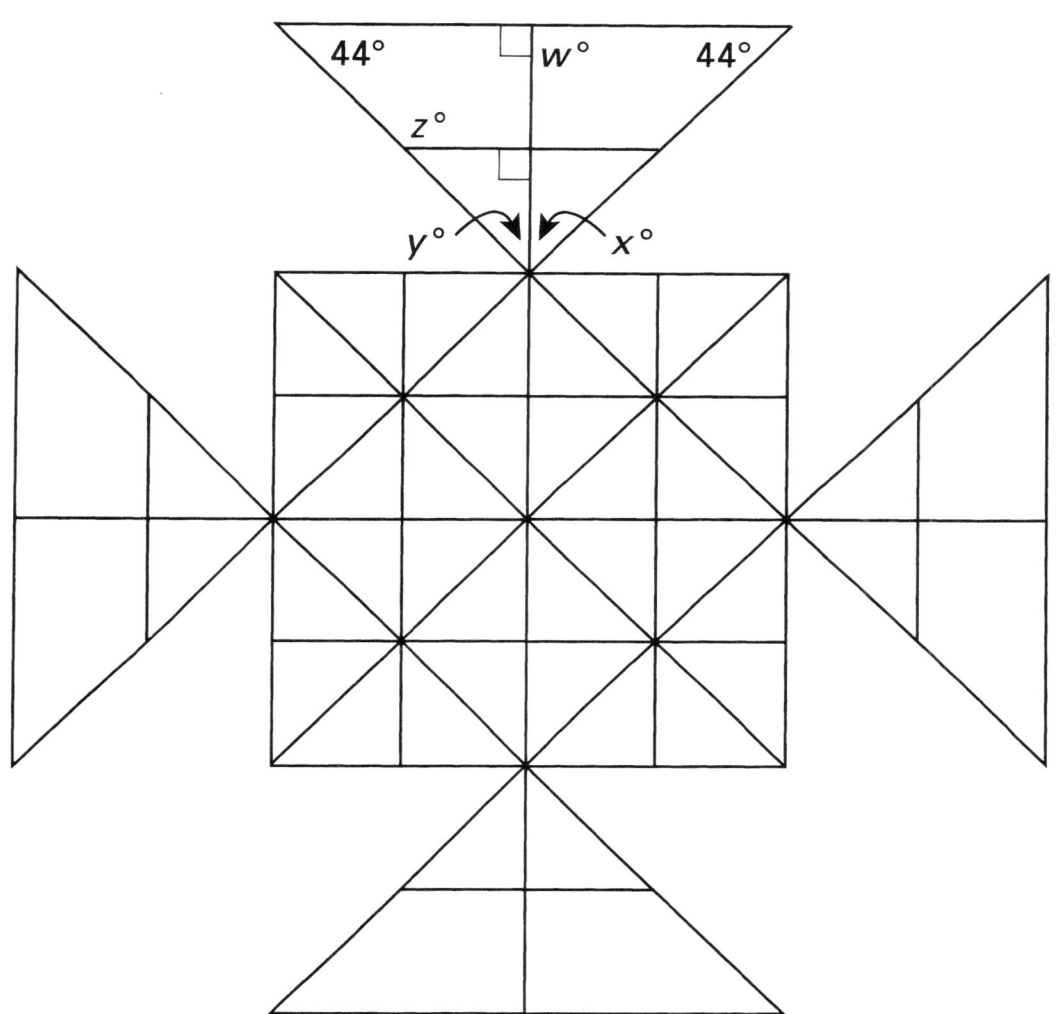

# Example 2

| Number of Copies<br>$n$ | Acme's Charges<br>$250 + 0.01n$ | Best's Charges<br>$70 + 0.03n$ |
|---|---|---|
| 0 | 250 | 70 |
| 2,000 | 270 | 130 |
| 4,000 | 290 | 190 |
| 6,000 | | |
| 8,000 | | |
| 10,000 | | |
| 12,000 | | |
| 14,000 | | |
| 16,000 | | |
| 18,000 | | |
| 20,000 | | |

# Question 30

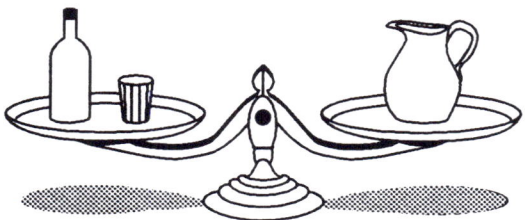

# Example 2

hare

| $t$ | $d = 5t$ |
|-----|----------|
| 0 | |
| 15 | |
| 30 | |

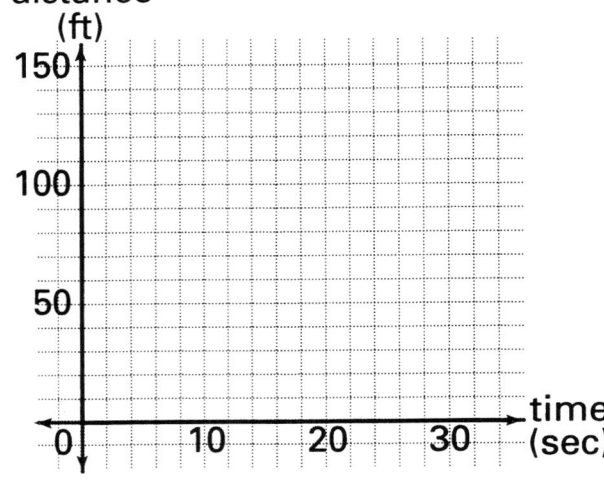

tortoise

| $t$ | $d = 100 + 0.1t$ |
|-----|------------------|
| 0 | |
| 15 | |
| 30 | |

---

# Question 10

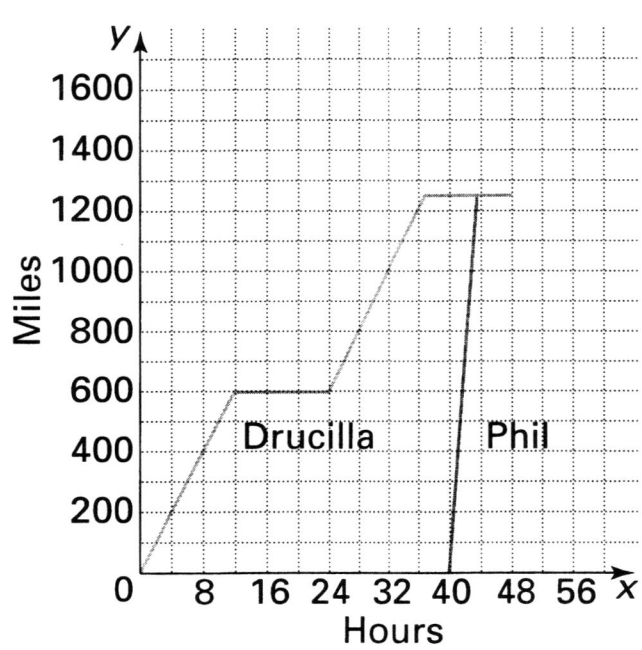

# Automatic Grapher Grids

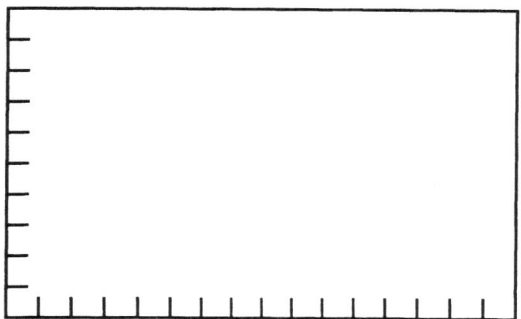

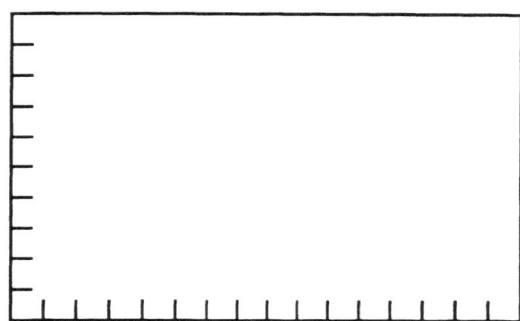

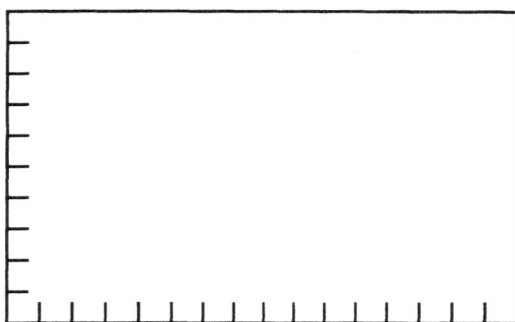

# Example 2

| $t$ number of years | height $h$ in ft | |
|---|---|---|
| | maple | beech |
| 0 | | |
| 2 | | |
| 4 | | |
| 6 | | |
| 8 | | |
| 10 | | |
| 12 | | |

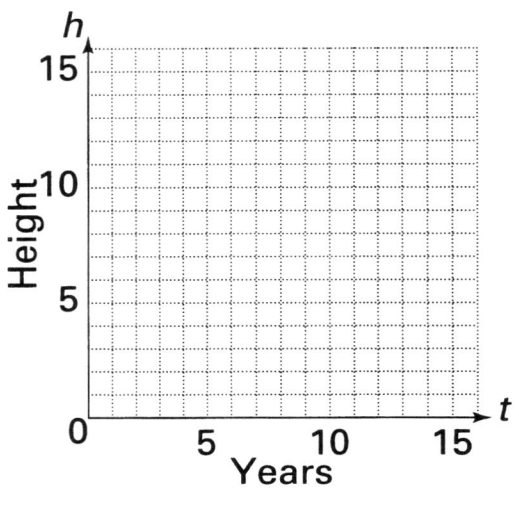

---

# Questions 5 and 6

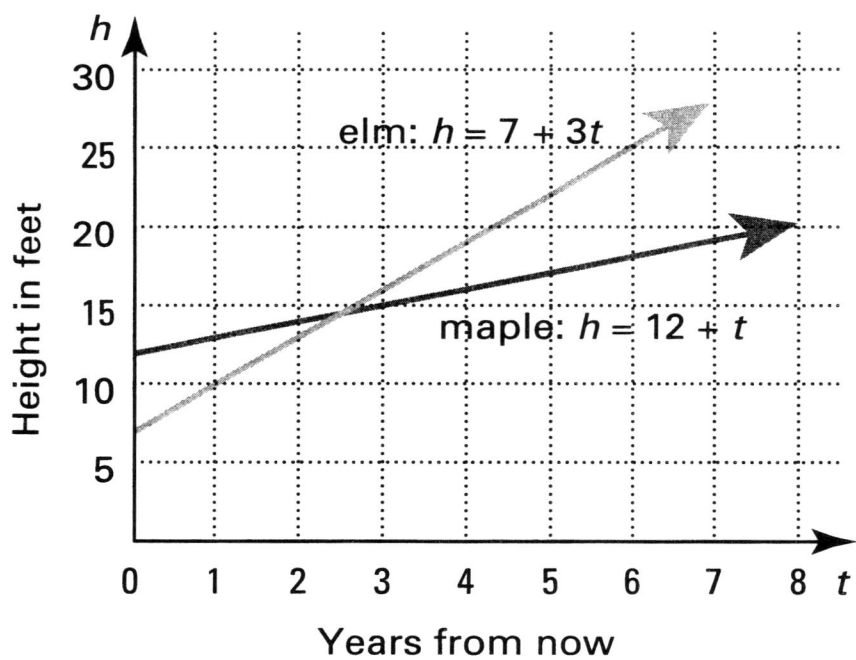

# Warm-up

Use the numbers to write two division sentences. Identify the quotient, dividend, and divisor in each sentence.

**1.** 6, 7, 42

**2.** 0.1, 10, 100

**3.** 6, $\frac{1}{2}$, 12

# Warm-up

The phrase *miles per hour* is an example of a rate unit. Notice that the units, miles and hours, are different. Write at least five other examples of rate units.

# Warm-up

Tim earned $12.50 for mowing a lawn. How many lawns did he mow if he earned

**1.** $62.50?

**2.** $100.00?

**3.** $125.00?

**4.** $187.50?

# Warm-up

**1.** Draw a spinner so that the probability of landing on either a 1, 2, 3, or 4 is $\frac{1}{4}$.

**2.** Draw a spinner so that the probability of landing on a 1 is $\frac{1}{8}$, a 2 is $\frac{1}{4}$, a 3 is $\frac{1}{2}$, and a 4 is $\frac{1}{8}$.

# Warm-up

Suppose 20% of a number is 73.

**1** What is 10% of the number?

**2.** What is 5% of the number?

**3.** What is 30% of the number?

**4.** What is 100% of the number?

**5.** What is 105% of the number?

# Warm-up

Find the area of each figure.

**1.** A circle with a radius of 6 cm

**2.** A square with sides of length 1.5 cm

**3.** A triangle with a height of 8 in. and a base of 16 in.

**4.** A circle with a diameter of 20 in.

**5.** A square with a perimeter of 24 in.

**6.** A rectangle with a length of $x$ cm and width of $2x$ cm

# Warm-up

Tell in which quadrant or on which axis the point lies.

|    | *x*-coordinate | *y*-coordinate |
|----|----------------|----------------|
| **1.** | positive | negative |
| **2.** | negative | negative |
| **3.** | negative | positive |
| **4.** | 0 | positive |
| **5.** | positive | positive |
| **6.** | negative | 0 |

# Warm-up

**1.** Write any two equal fractions. Show that the fractions satisfy the Means-Extremes Property.

**2.** Write any two unequal fractions. Show that the fractions do not satisfy the Means-Extremes Property.

**3.** Are the fractions $\frac{14}{49}$ and $\frac{18}{56}$ equal? Explain your answer.

**4.** Three apples cost 60¢. How much will a dozen apples cost?

# Warm-up

Write a problem that could be solved using the following proportions.

**1.** $\frac{1}{200} = \frac{2.5}{n}$    **2.** $\frac{12}{30} = \frac{n}{40}$

# Question 34

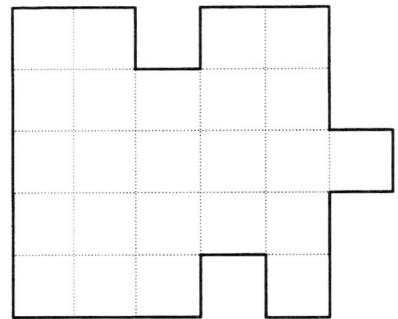

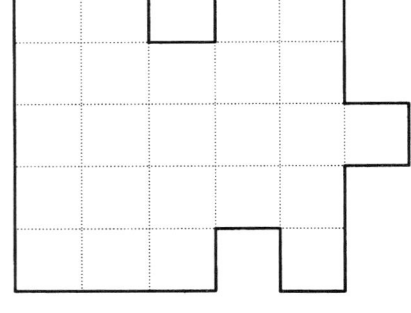

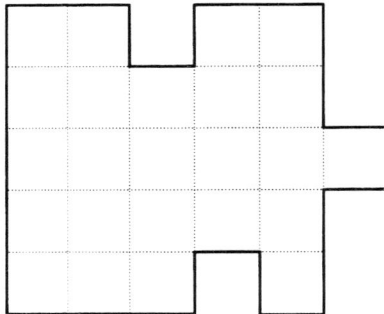

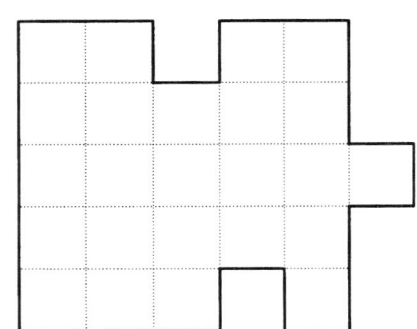

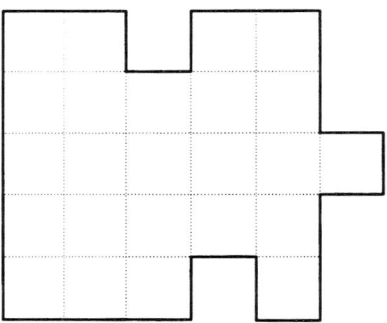

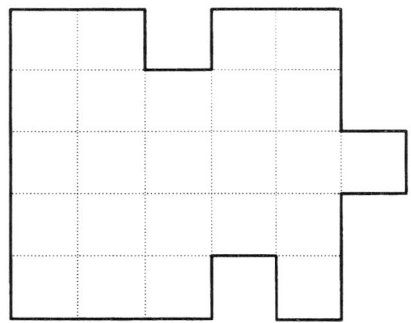

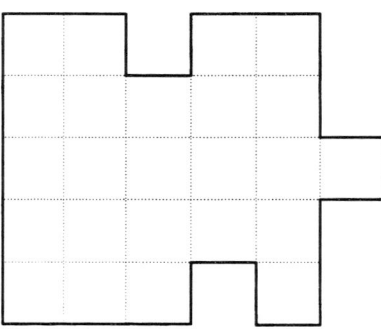

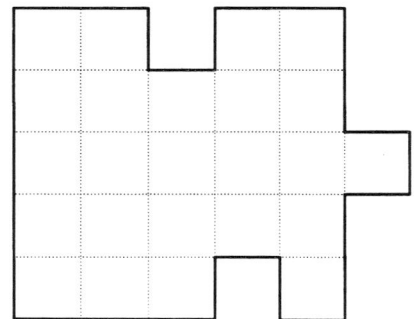

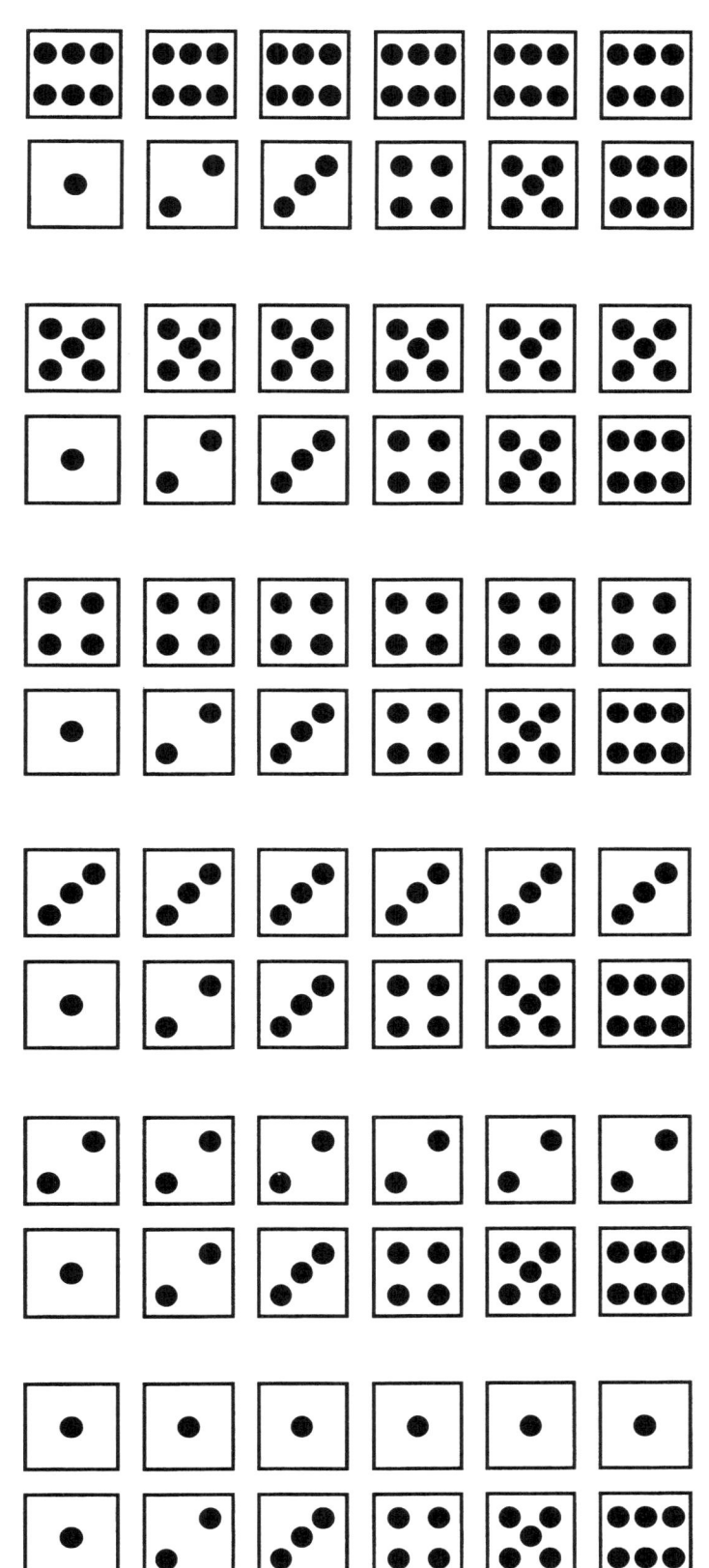

**Two-Dice Outcomes**

# Relative Frequency and Probability

| Relative Frequency | Probability |
|---|---|
| 1. calculated from an experiment | 1. deduced from assumptions (like randomness) or assumed to be close to some relative frequency |
| 2. the ratio of the number of times an event has occurred to the number of times it could occur | 2. if outcomes are equally likely, the ratio of the number of outcomes in an event to the total number of possible outcomes |
| 3. 0 means that an event did not occur. 1 means the event occurred every time it could. | 3. 0 means that an event is impossible. 1 means that an event is sure to happen. |
| 4. The more often an event occurred relative to the number of times it could occur, the closer its relative frequency is to 1. | 4. The more likely an event is, the closer its probability is to 1. |
| 5. If the relative frequency of an event is $r$, then the relative frequency of its complement is $1 - r$. | 5. If the probability of an event is $p$, then the probability of its complement is $1 - p$. |

# Examples 1–4

## Example 1

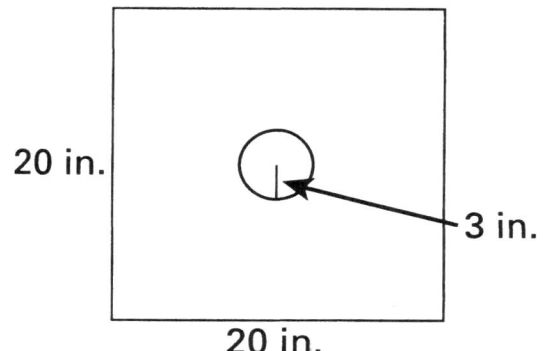

20 in.

3 in.

20 in.

## Example 2

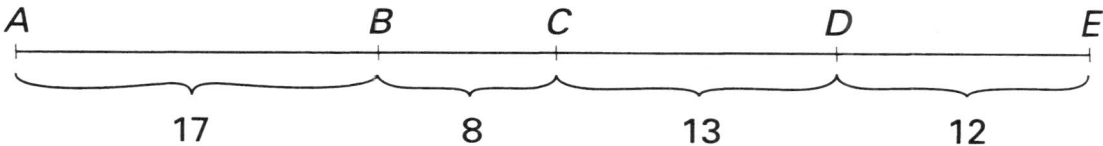

A         B     C     D     E

17     8     13     12

## Example 3        Example 4

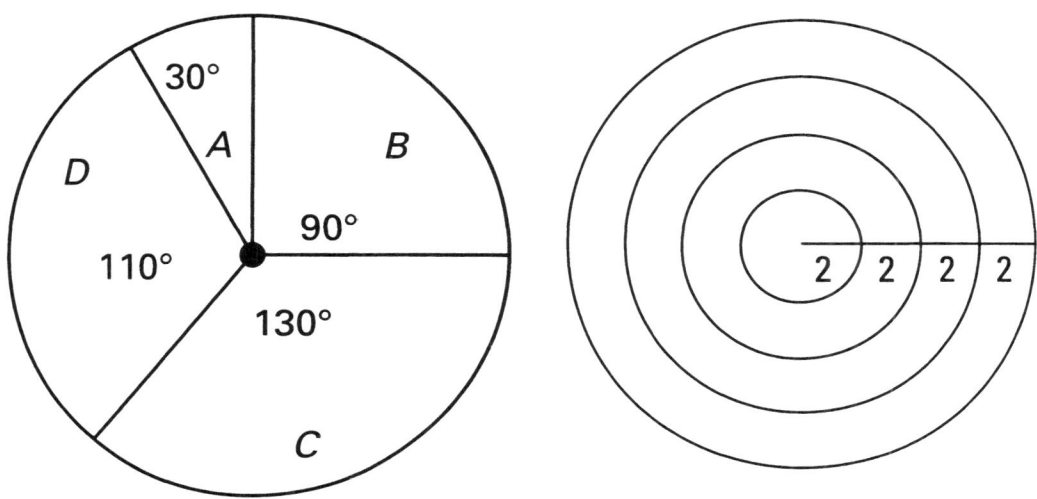

30°

A   B

90°

110°

130°

C

D

2 2 2 2

# Additional Examples

**1.** A round dart board has a large bull's-eye of radius 5. The board has a radius of 15. If a dart lands randomly on any point of the board, what is the probability that it will land on the bull's eye?

**2.** The Roadrunner runs down a mile-long stretch of highway. He stops once at random. If the Roadrunner stops on the 100-foot section patrolled by the Coyote, the Coyote will chase him. What is the probability that this will happen?

**3.** A spinner is equally likely to land at any position on a dial. In the diagram at the right, what is the probability that it lands in region *B*? in region *C* or *D*?

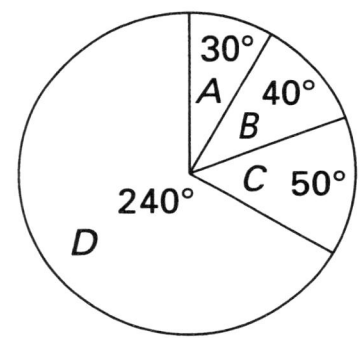

**4.** In the square at the right, everything outside the triangle has been shaded. If a point is chosen at random, what is the probability that it will lie in the shaded portion? (Remember that the area of a triangle = $\frac{1}{2}$ • base • height.)

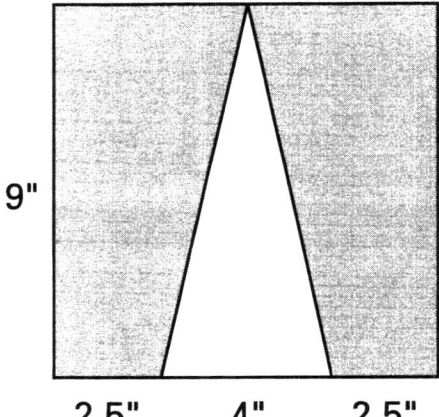

# Questions 11, 13 and 14

**11.**

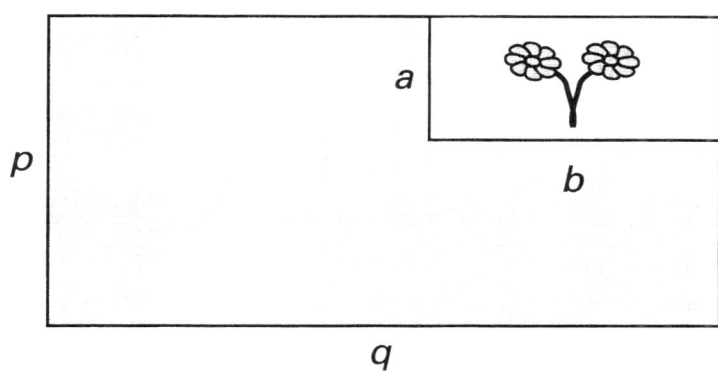

**13.**

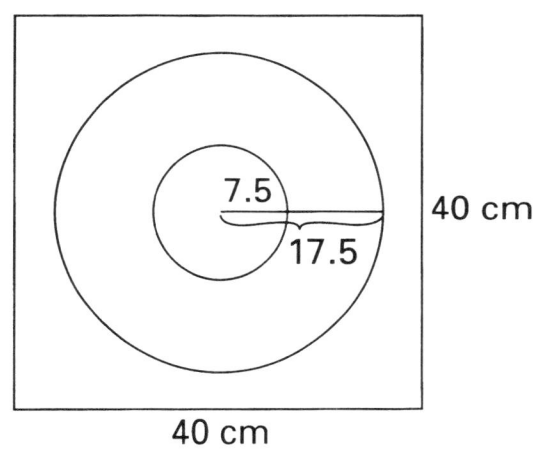

**14.**

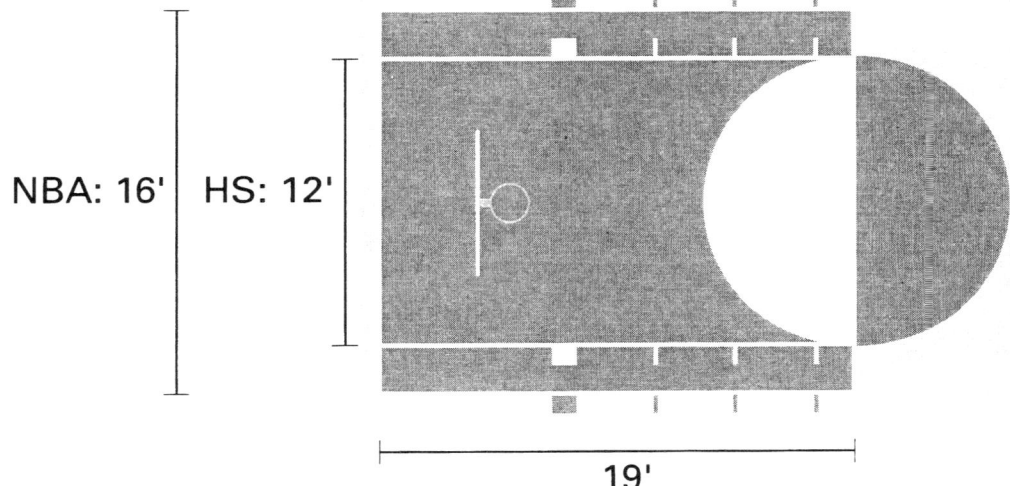

# Challenge

Solve the following problem. A kidney-shaped swimming pool is located in a rectangular back yard. The sides of the pool consist of four connecting semicircles. A parachutist is hired to land in the back yard during a party. Assuming the parachutist lands somewhere in the back yard, what is the probability he or she will land on dry land?

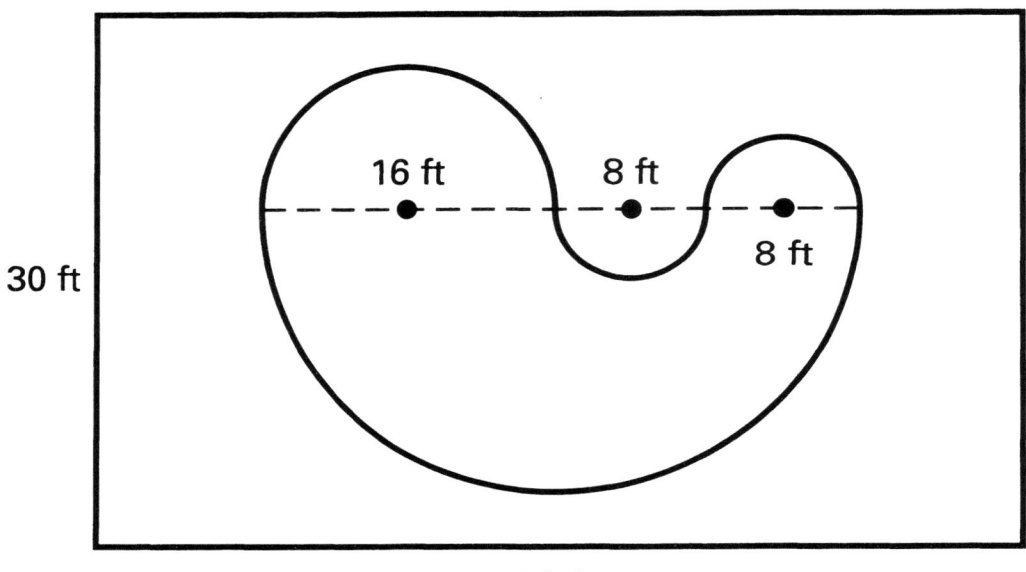

16 ft  8 ft  8 ft

30 ft

50 ft

# Example 2

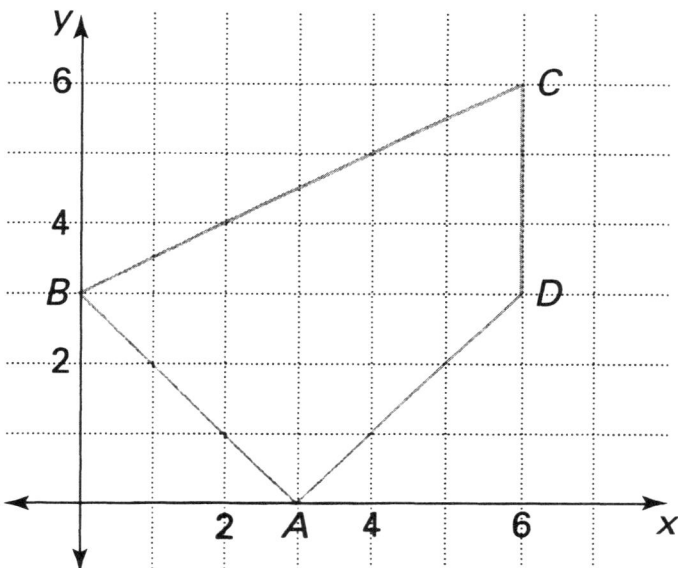

# Example 3

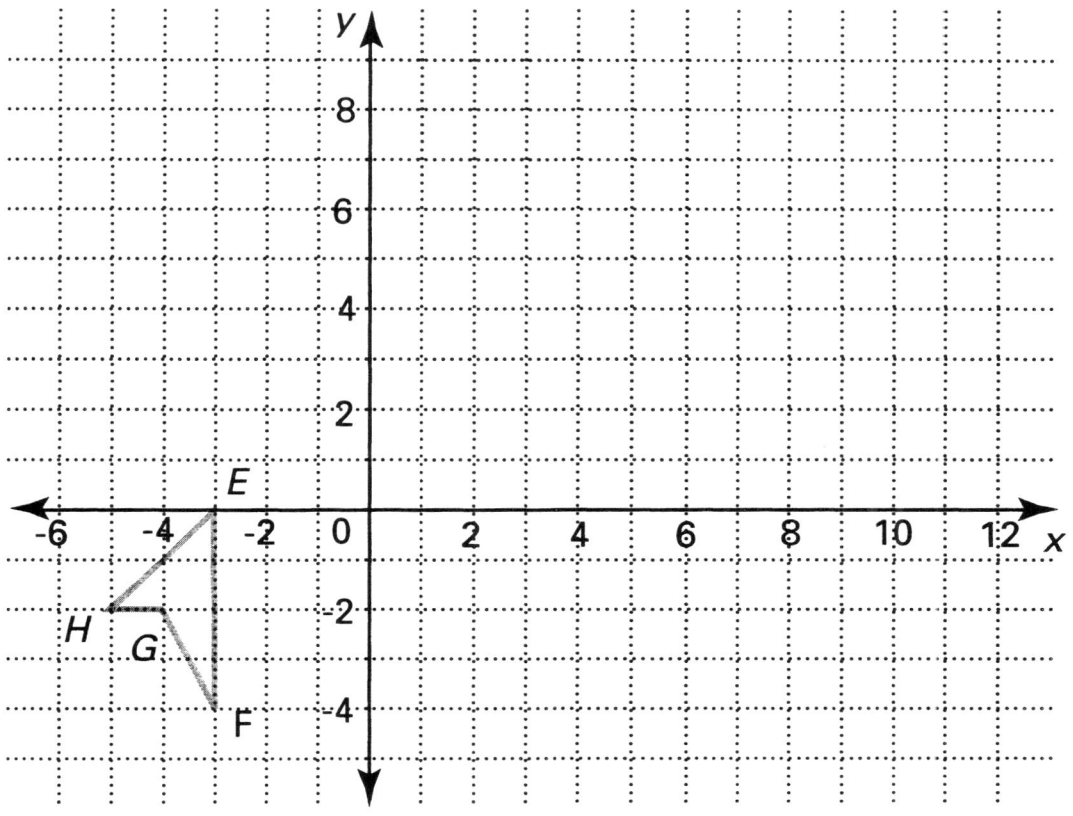

# Similar Figures

| △ ABC | △ A'B'C' | Ratios | △ A"B"C" | Ratios |
|---|---|---|---|---|
| AB | A'B' | | A"B" | |
| BC | B'C' | | B"C" | |
| AC | A'C' | | A"C" | |
| m∠A | m∠A' | | m∠A" | |
| m∠B | m∠B' | | m∠B" | |
| m∠C | m∠C' | | m∠C" | |

| Quadrilateral WXYZ | Quadrilateral W'X'Y'Z' | Ratios |
|---|---|---|
| WX | W'X' | |
| XY | X'Y' | |
| YZ | Y'Z' | |
| WZ | W'Z' | |
| m∠W | m∠W' | |
| m∠X | m∠X' | |
| m∠Y | m∠Y' | |
| m∠Z | m∠Z' | |

# Additional Examples

**1.** The quadrilaterals are similar with corresponding sides parallel.
   **a.** Find $x$ and $y$.
   **b.** What are the two possible ratios of similitude for the figures?

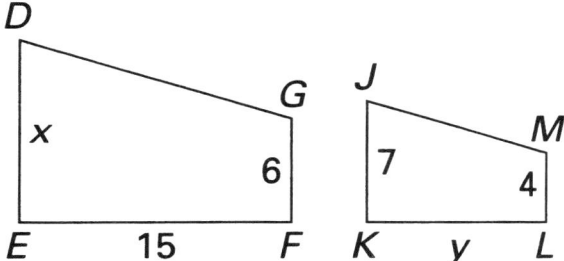

**2.** A vase is sold in two sizes. The small vase is similar to the large vase. Find the height of the small vase.

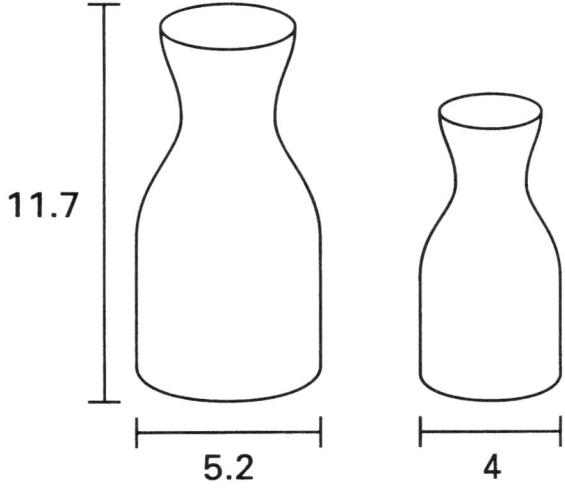

# Questions 8, 12 and 13

**8.**

**12.**

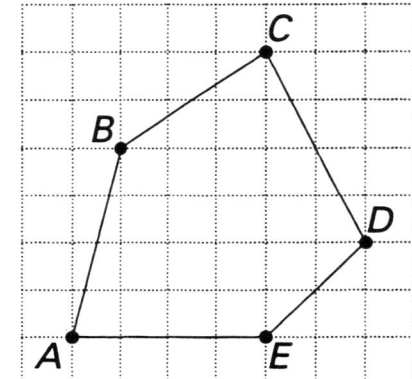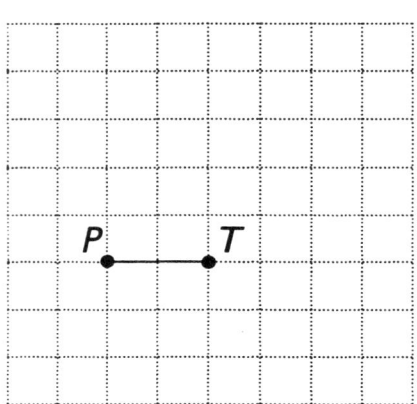

**13.**

# Warm-up

Refer to page 417. Write a paragraph describing the changes in Manhattan's population from 1790 to 1990.

# Warm-up

Find the value of $y$ in each equation for the given value of $x$.

**1.** $2x + 5y = 12$; $x = 1$     **2.** $2x + 5y = 12$; $x = 0$

**3.** $6x - 3y = 21$; $x = 0$     **4.** $6x - 3y = 21$; $x = -1$

Find the value of $x$ in each equation for the given value of $y$.

**5.** $x + y = 7$; $y = 0$     **6.** $x + y = 7$; $y = 2$

**7.** $4x - y = 11$; $y = 1$     **8.** $4x - y = 11$; $y = 0$

# Warm-up

The roof of a building has a pitch of $\frac{7}{12}$. This means that the roof rises 7 feet when the horizontal distance from the top is 12 feet.

**1.** Point $R$ is on the roof and its horizontal distance from the top is 24 feet. What is its vertical distance from the top?

**2.** Point $T$ is on the roof and its vertical distance from the top is 10.5 feet. What is its horizontal distance from the top?

# Warm-up

Find the slope of a line through the given pair of points.

**1.** (6, 4) and (2, 1)

**2.** (5, 7) and (5, 12)

**3.** (-4, 6) and (2, -6)

**4.** (2, 4) and (6, 2)

**5.** (-3, 8) and (5, 8)

# Warm-up

Tell if the sentence is *true* or *false.*

**1.** Equations of every line can be written in slope-intercept form.

**2.** One line with a slope of 3 is $y = 3x - 2$.

**3.** The slope of every horizontal line is 0.

**4.** Zero is always the *x*-coordinate of a *y*-intercept.

**5.** The graph of a line with a negative slope goes downward from left to right.

# Warm-up

For a service call, a plumbing company charges a base rate plus $20 for each quarter-hour of service or fraction thereof. A $1\frac{1}{2}$ hour service call costs $155.

**1.** What is the base rate charged by the company?

**2.** Write an equation relating the cost of a service call *y* to the number of quarter-hours of service *x.*

# Warm-up

Write a paragraph about the information given in the graph below. Include some predictions about attendance in the years that are not shown on the graph.

Number of Freshmen at Wilson High (1988–1994)

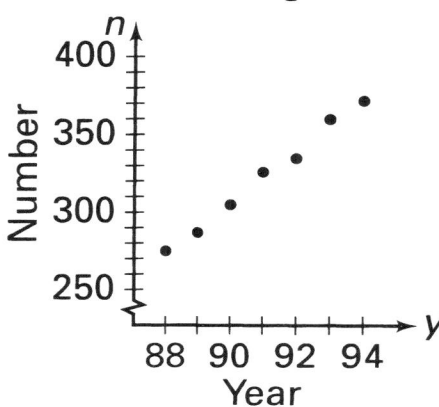

# Warm-up

Softball caps cost $10 and team shirts cost $15. A total of $630, excluding tax, was spent on caps and shirts. Name five different combinations of caps and shirts that could have been ordered.

# Warm-up

Graph each equation.

**1.** $x = 3$

**2.** $y = -2$

**3.** $x = 0$

**4.** $y = -3x + 2$

# Population of Manhattan Island

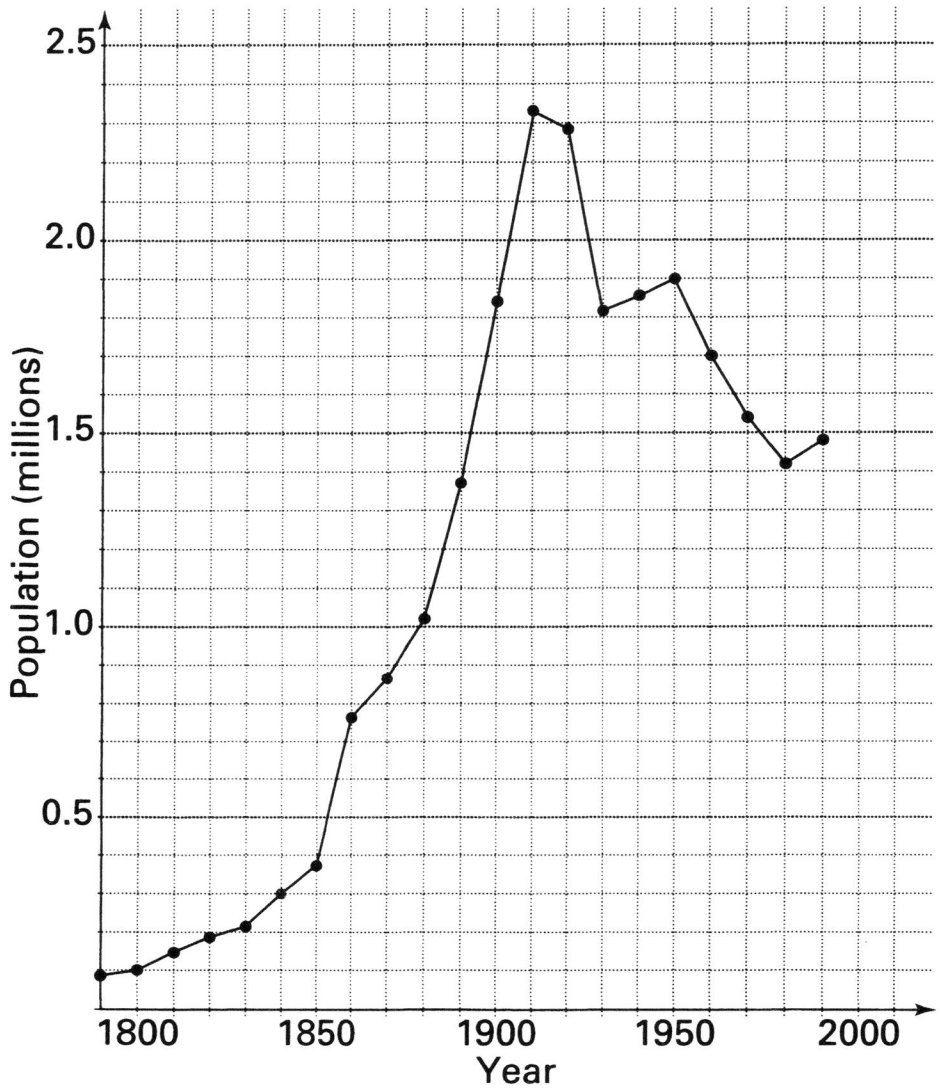

| Year | Population | Year | Population |
|------|-----------|------|-----------|
| 1900 | 1,850,093 | 1970 | 1,539,233 |
| 1910 | 2,331,542 | 1980 | 1,428,285 |
| 1920 | 2,284,103 | 1990 | 1,487,536 |
| 1960 | 1,698,281 | | |

# Manhattan Spreadsheet

|    | A    | B          | C                     |
|----|------|------------|-----------------------|
| 1  |      |            | Rate of Change        |
| 2  | Year | Population | for Previous Decade   |
| 3  | 1900 | 1850093    |                       |
| 4  | 1910 | 2331542    | 48144.9               |
| 5  | 1920 | 2284103    | -4743.9               |
| 6  | 1930 | 1876412    |                       |
| 7  | 1940 | 1889924    |                       |
| 8  | 1950 | 1960101    |                       |
| 9  | 1960 | 1698281    |                       |
| 10 | 1970 | 1539233    |                       |
| 11 | 1980 | 1428285    |                       |
| 12 | 1990 | 1487536    |                       |

## Additional Examples

**1.** The chart below shows Tom's income
for each week of a six-week period.

| Week | 1 | 2 | 3 | 4 | 5 | 6 |
|---|---|---|---|---|---|---|
| Dollars | 11 | 15 | 0 | 21 | 25 | 25 |

**a.** Graph these points and connect
them.

**b.** Find the rate of change of Tom's
income between weeks 1 and 6.

**c.** During what time period was the
rate of change of income
negative? How can you tell?

**d.** When was the rate of change 0?
How can you tell?

**2.** The graph shows the
weight of Li-Li, the first
giant panda born in
captivity, at age
1 month, 3 months,
and 6 months.

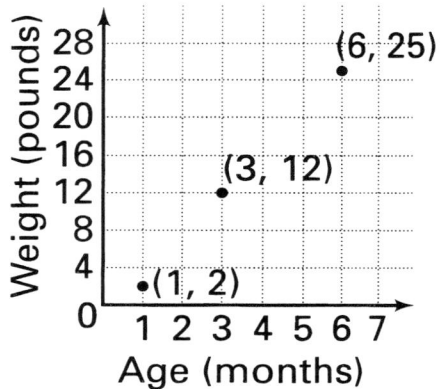

**a.** Find the rate of
change in weight
per month from 1 month to 3 months
and from 3 months to 6 months.

**b.** During which time period did Li-
Li's weight increase faster?

# Questions 14–17

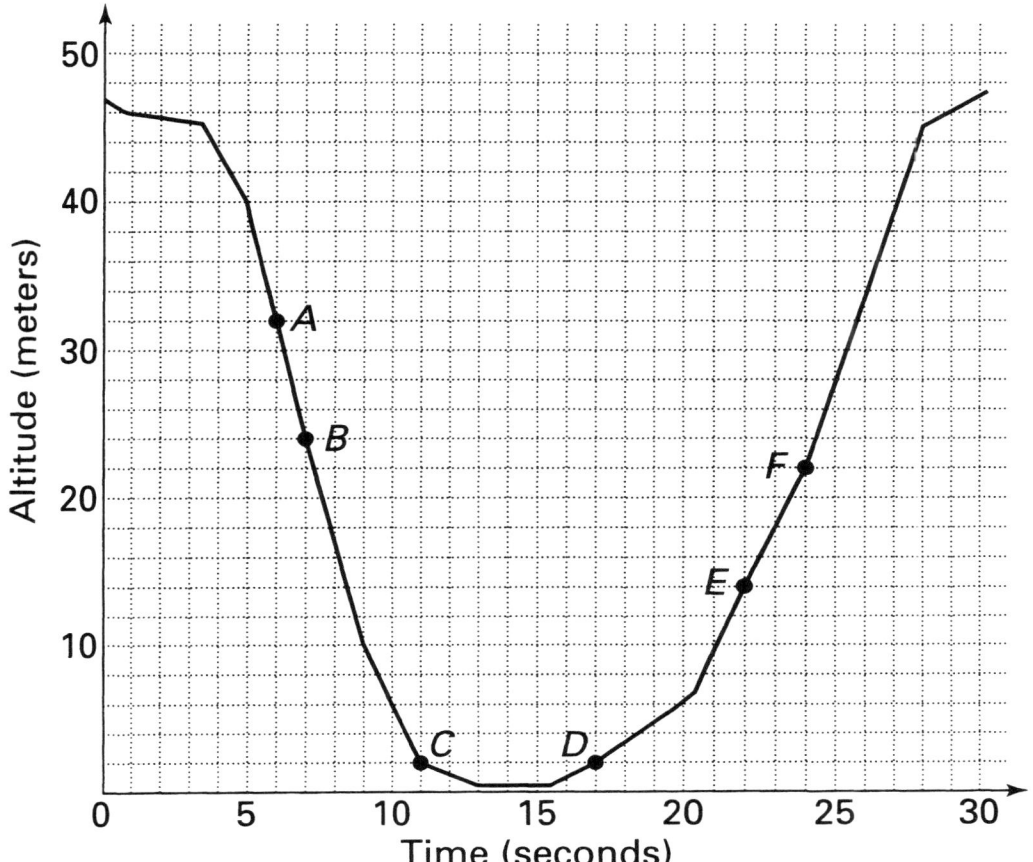

# Example 2

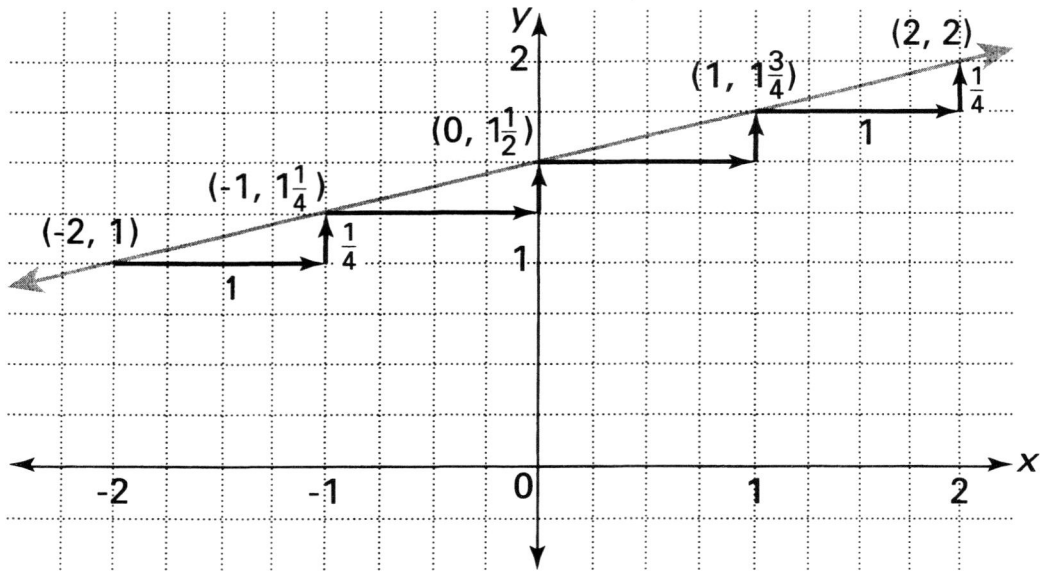

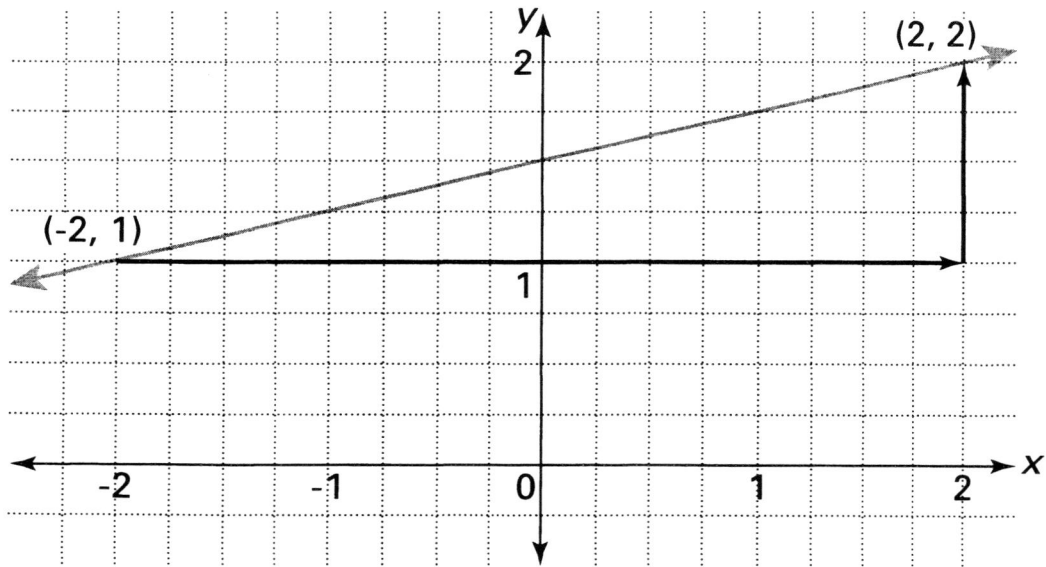

# Questions 5–6, 16–18

**5.**

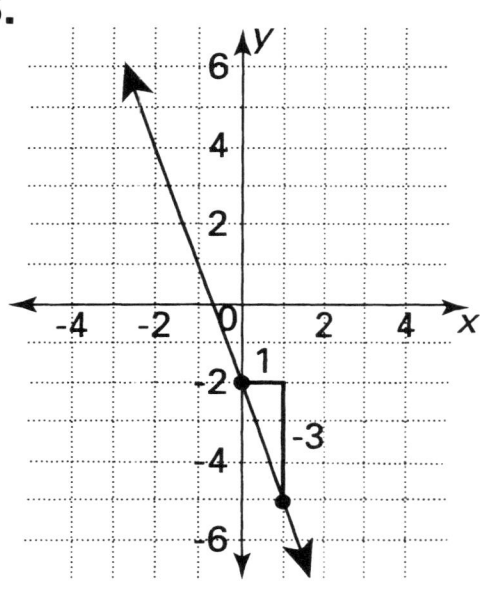

**6.**

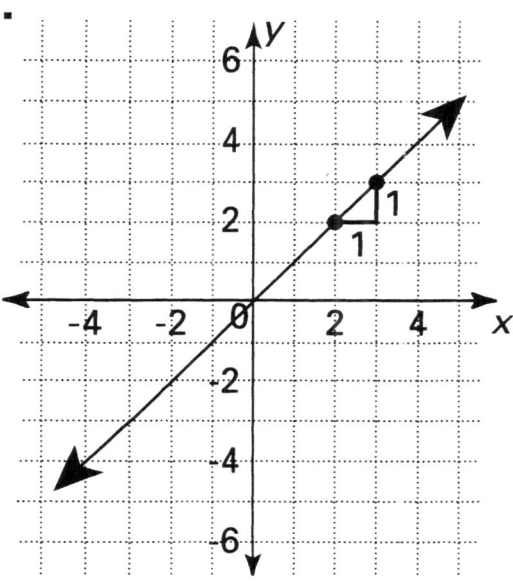

**16.** Slope = 7

|   | A | B |
|---|---|---|
| 1 | x | y |
| 2 | -5 | 2 |
| 3 | -4 |   |
| 4 | -3 |   |
| 5 | -2 |   |

**17.** Slope = -8

|   | A | B |
|---|---|---|
| 1 | x | y |
| 2 | 6 | 10 |
| 3 | 7 |   |
| 4 | 8 |   |
| 5 | 9 |   |

**18.** Slope = $\frac{5}{4}$

|   | A | B |
|---|---|---|
| 1 | x | y |
| 2 | 0 | 2 |
| 3 | 1 |   |
| 4 | 2 |   |
| 5 | 3 |   |

# Questions 26–28

## Average Home Runs per Game

| Year | American League | National League |
|------|-----------------|-----------------|
| 1981 | 1.42 | 1.12 |
| 1982 | 1.83 | 1.34 |
| 1983 | 1.68 | 1.44 |
| 1984 | 1.75 | 1.32 |
| 1985 | 1.93 | 1.47 |
| 1986 | 2.02 | 1.57 |
| 1987 | 2.32 | 1.88 |
| 1988 | 1.68 | 1.32 |
| 1989 | 1.51 | 1.41 |
| 1990 | 1.59 | 1.56 |
| 1991 | 1.72 | 1.47 |
| 1992 | 1.57 | 1.30 |
| 1993 | 1.83 | 1.72 |

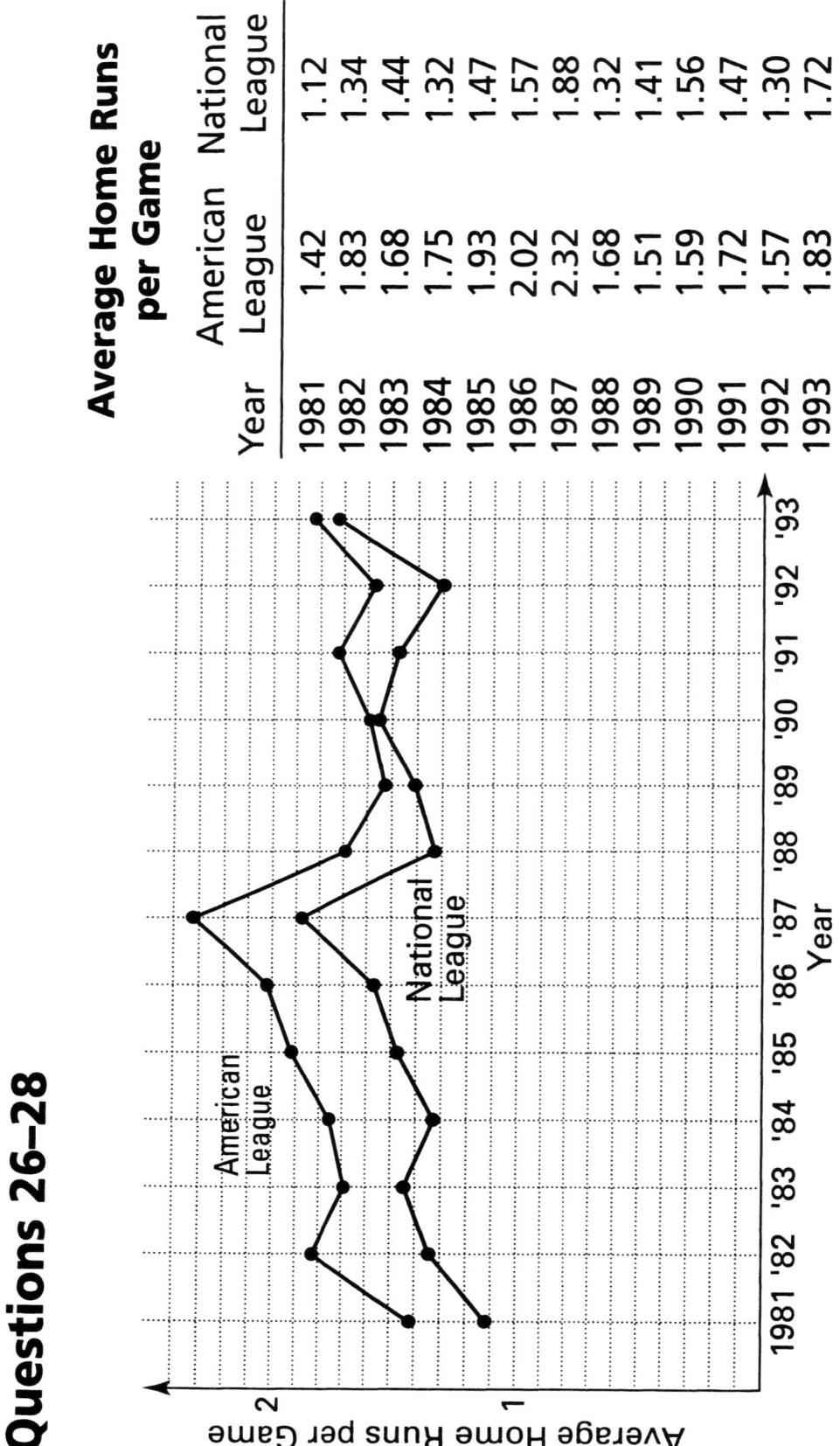

# Latitude and Temperature

| City | North Latitude | April Mean High Temperature (°F) |
|---|---|---|
| Lagos, Nigeria | 6 | 89 |
| San Juan, Puerto Rico | 18 | 84 |
| Calcutta, India | 23 | 97 |
| Cairo, Egypt | 30 | 83 |
| Tokyo, Japan | 35 | 63 |
| Rome, Italy | 42 | 68 |
| Quebec City, Canada | 47 | 46 |
| London, England | 52 | 56 |
| Copenhagen, Denmark | 56 | 50 |
| Moscow, Russia | 56 | 47 |

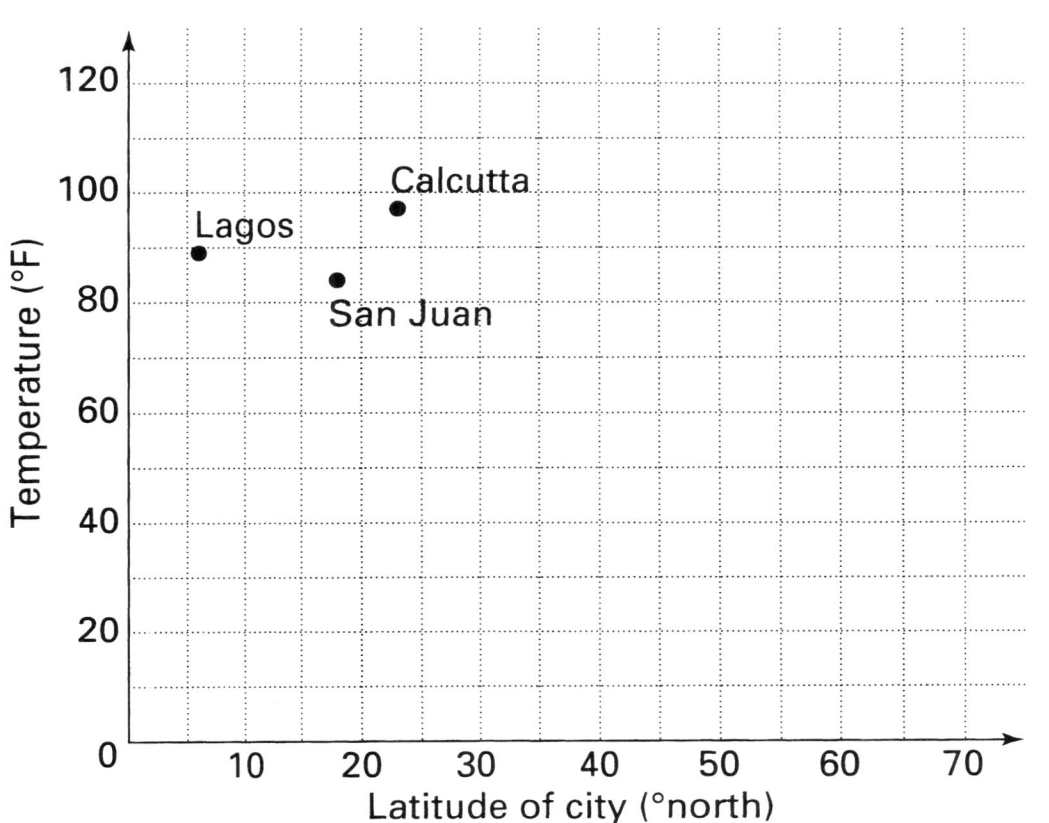

# Additional Examples

**1.** The table shows the amount of gold that was mined in the world for the years 1984 to 1992.

| Gold Production: 1984–1992 (millions of troy ounces) | |
| --- | --- |
| 1984: 46.9 | 1989: 65.3 |
| 1985: 49.3 | 1990: 68.6 |
| 1986: 51.5 | 1991: 69.1 |
| 1987: 51.5 | 1992: 72.2 |
| 1988: 60.3 | |

**a.** Draw a scatterplot.

**b.** Use a ruler to fit a line to the data.

**c.** Write an equation for the line.

**2.** Use your equation in Question **1c** to predict the amount of gold that will be mined in the year 2000.

# Questions 12–15

**12.**

**13.**

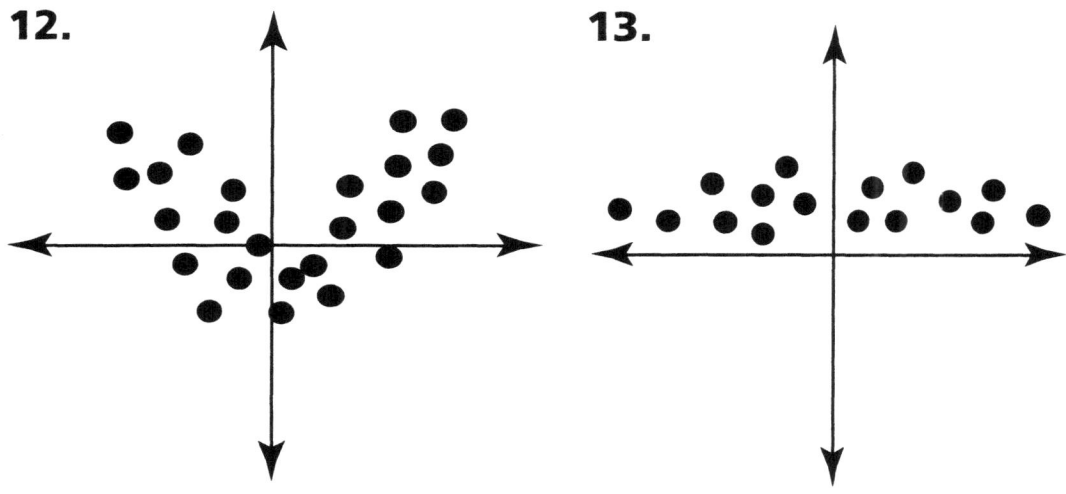

**14.**

**15.**

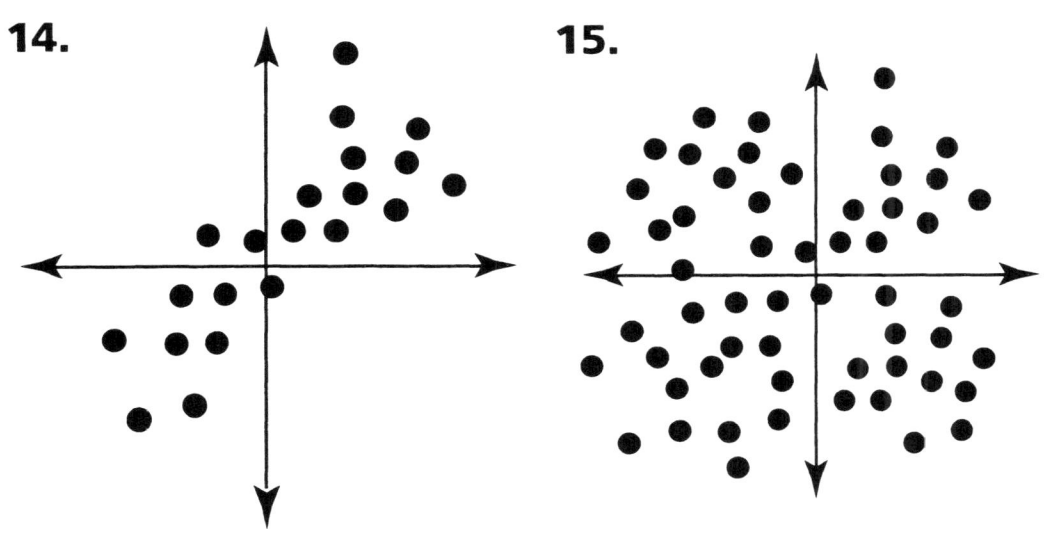

# Question 16

| City | North Latitude | January Mean Low Temperature (°F) |
|---|---|---|
| Lagos, Nigeria | 6 | 74 |
| San Juan, Puerto Rico | 18 | 67 |
| Calcutta, India | 23 | 55 |
| Cairo, Egypt | 30 | 47 |
| Tokyo, Japan | 35 | 29 |
| Rome, Italy | 42 | 39 |
| Quebec City, Canada | 47 | 2 |
| London, England | 52 | 35 |
| Copenhagen, Denmark | 56 | 29 |
| Moscow, Russia | 56 | 9 |

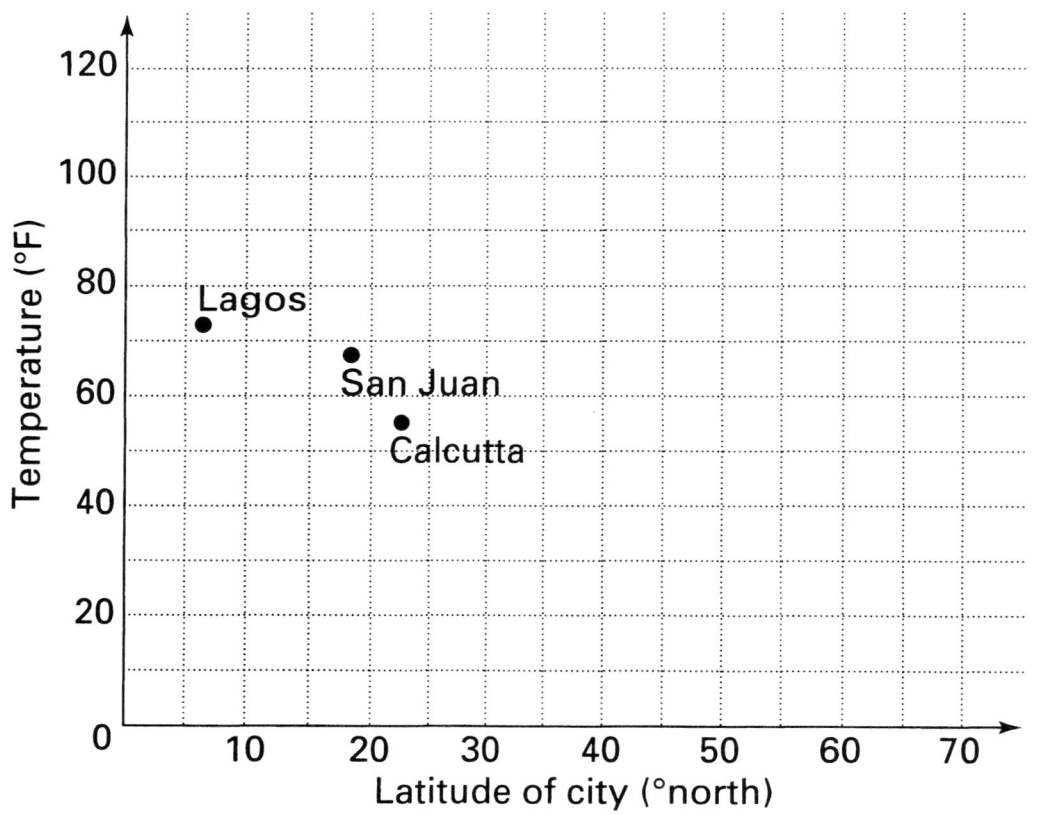

# Additional Examples

**1.** Graph all ordered pairs $(x, y)$ that satisfy $y \geq 4$.

**2.** Give a sentence describing all points in each shaded region.

**a.**

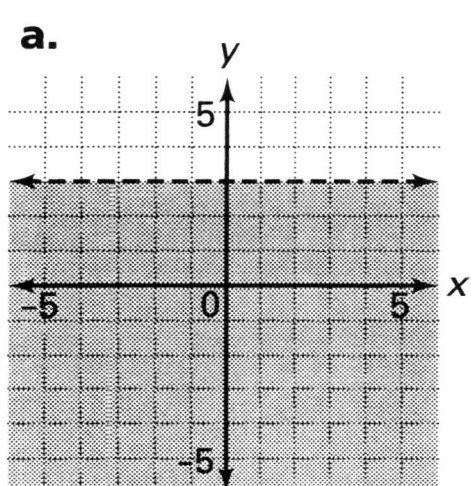

**b.**

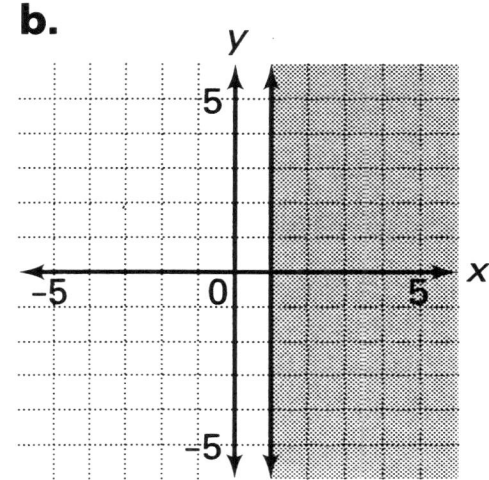

**3.** Graph $y < 3x - 4$.

**4.** Graph $2x + 5y \geq 10$.

**5.** Suppose crepe paper costs $2.00 per package, and balloons are $1.50 per pack. The decorations committee for the dance bought some of each and stayed within their $60 budget. Graph the possible number of packages of each that they could have bought. Let $b$ represent the number of packs of balloons and $c$ represent the number of packages of crepe paper.

# Question 24

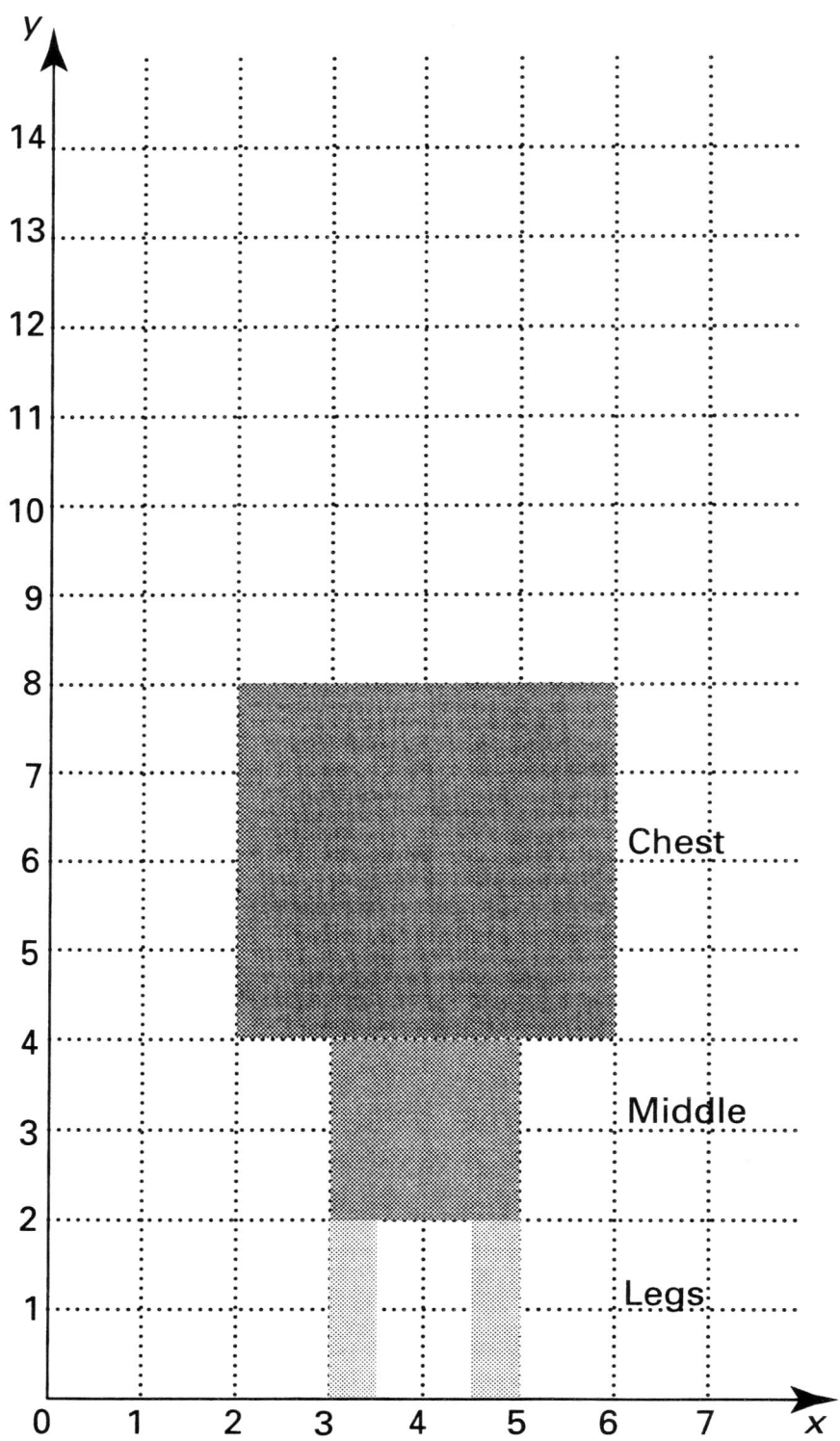

# Warm-up

Write each percent as a decimal.

**1.** 3%          **2.** $5\frac{1}{2}$%          **3.** 10%

**4.** 8.5%          **5.** 2.75%

# Warm-up

Find the value of each term for
$x = 0, 1, 2, 3, \ldots 10$.

**1.** $2^x$          **2.** $25 \cdot 2^x$          **3.** $3 \cdot 2^x$

# Warm-up

Work with a partner to solve the following problem.

Seth told Joey that a small bug, which weighs 0.05 of an ounce, will double its weight every day for two weeks. Should Joey believe Seth? Explain your answer.

# Warm-up

Fill in each blank with >, <, or = to make the sentence true.

**1.** $3^2$ ___ $2^3$          **2.** $4^0$ ___ $2^2$          **3.** $\left(\frac{1}{2}\right)^2$ ___ $\left(\frac{1}{4}\right)^2$

**4.** $6^0$ ___ $\left(\frac{1}{3}\right)^0$          **5.** $.5^3$ ___ $\left(\frac{1}{2}\right)^3$          **6.** $.7^4$ ___ $.7^3$

**7.** $50(.8)^5$ ___ $50(.8)^6$          **8.** $50(1.4)^5$ ___ $50(1.4)^6$

# Warm-up

Name the numbers described.
1. Doubling this number gives the same result as squaring it.

2. Any nonzero number raised to this power is equal to one.

3. This number raised to any whole-number power equals one.

4. This number raised to the zero power is undefined.

# Warm-up

1. Write the values of the integer powers of 10 from $10^{-6}$ to $10^6$.

2. Multiply.
   **a.** $10^{-7} \times 10^7$      **b.** $10^{-4} \times 10^4$

   **c.** $10^{-2} \times 10^2$      **d.** $10^{-1} \times 10^1$

3. What is true for each pair of numbers in Question 2?

# Warm-up

1. Find the values of $3^n$ for integer values of $n$ from -8 to 8.

Use your answers to Question 1 to help you write each product as a product of powers.

**2.** $\frac{1}{243} \cdot 6561 = 27$    **3.** $729 \cdot \frac{1}{81} = 9$    **4.** $\frac{1}{27} \cdot \frac{1}{9} = \frac{1}{243}$

**5.** $\frac{1}{2187} \cdot 3 = \frac{1}{729}$      **6.** $243 \cdot 27 = 6561$

# Warm-up

If a large cube-shaped crate is completely filled with 27 identical small cube-shaped boxes, what is the relationship between the length of a side of the crate and the length of a side of a small box?

# Warm-up

Write the algebraic description of each property. Then give an example that illustrates each property.

**1.** Quotient of Powers Property

**2.** Zero Exponent Property

**3.** Product of Powers Property

**4.** Power of a Product Property

**5.** Negative Exponent Property

**6.** Power of a Quotient Property

**7.** Power of a Power Property

# Population Growth

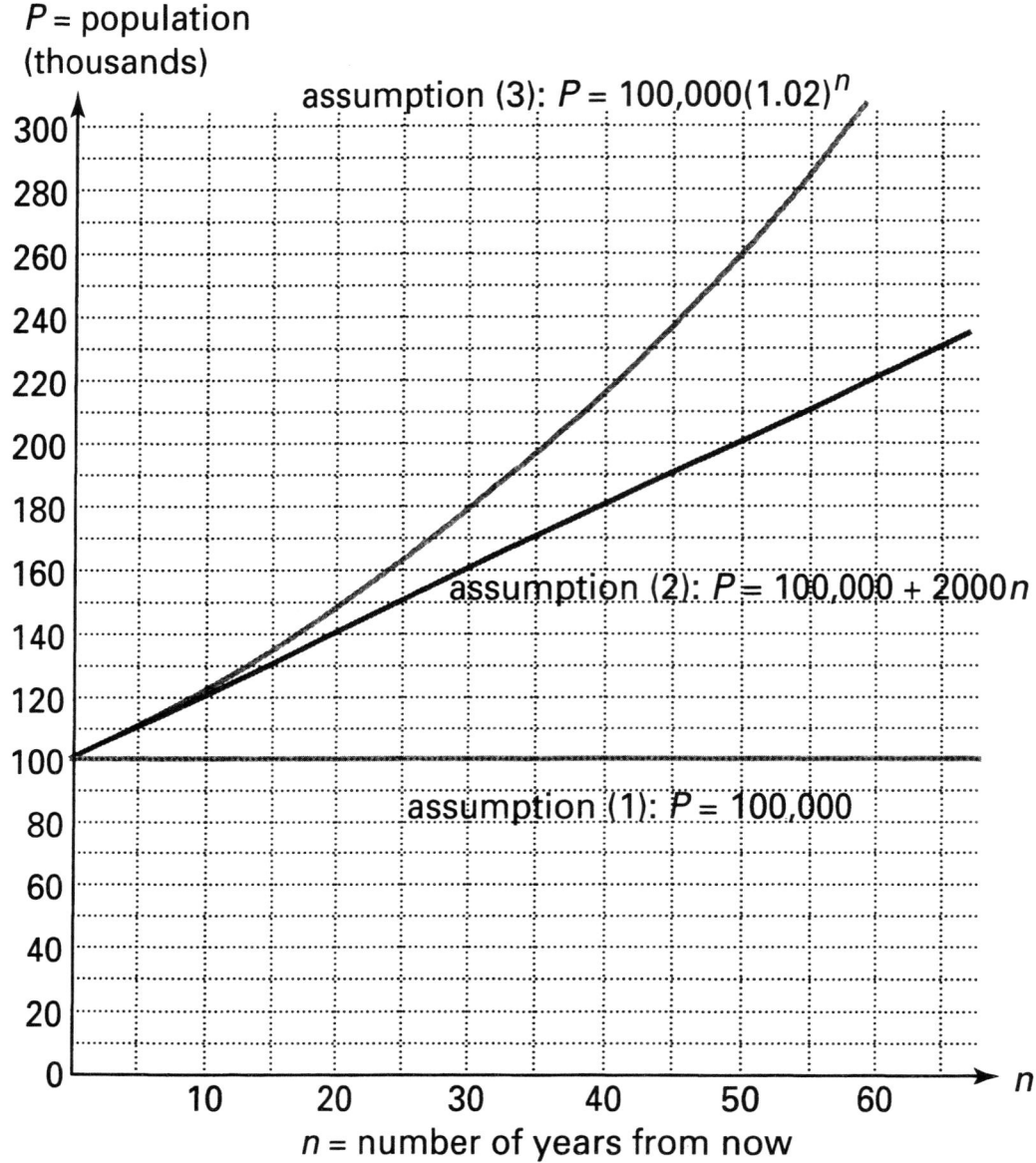

$P$ = population
(thousands)

assumption (3): $P = 100{,}000(1.02)^n$

assumption (2): $P = 100{,}000 + 2000n$

assumption (1): $P = 100{,}000$

$n$ = number of years from now

# Example 1

| | Option (1):<br>add 50 | Option (2):<br>multiply by 1.5 |
|---|---|---|
| 1st day | $10 + 50 \cdot 1 = \$ 60$ | $10 \cdot 1.5^1 = \$ 15.00$ |
| 2nd day | $10 + 50 \cdot 2 = \$110$ | $10 \cdot 1.5^2 = \$ 22.50$ |
| 3rd day | $10 + 50 \cdot 3 = \$160$ | $10 \cdot 1.5^3 = \$ 33.75$ |
| 4th day | $10 + 50 \cdot 4 = \$210$ | $10 \cdot 1.5^4 \approx \$ 50.63$ |
| 5th day | $10 + 50 \cdot 5 = \$260$ | $10 \cdot 1.5^5 \approx \$ 75.94$ |
| 6th day | $10 + 50 \cdot 6 = \$310$ | $10 \cdot 1.5^6 \approx \$113.91$ |
| 7th day | $10 + 50 \cdot 7 = \$360$ | $10 \cdot 1.5^7 \approx \$170.86$ |
| $\bullet$ | $\bullet$ | $\bullet$ |
| $\bullet$ | $\bullet$ | $\bullet$ |
| $\bullet$ | $\bullet$ | $\bullet$ |
| $n$th day | $10 + 50n$ | $10 \cdot 1.5^n$ |

# Constant Increase and Exponential Growth

| **Constant Increase** | **Exponential Growth** |
|---|---|
| **1.** Begin with an amount *b*. | **1.** Begin with an amount *b*. |
| **2.** *Add m* (the slope) in each of *x* time periods. | **2.** *Multiply* by *g* (the growth factor) in each of *x* time periods. |
| **3.** After the *x* time periods, there will be *b* + *mx*. | **3.** After the *x* time periods, the amount will be *b* • *g^x*. |

### Constant Increase

$y = mx + b, \ m > 0$

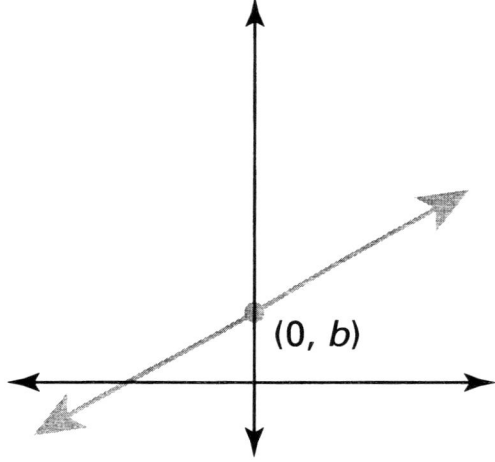

(0, *b*)

### Exponential Growth

$y = b \cdot g^x, \ g > 1$

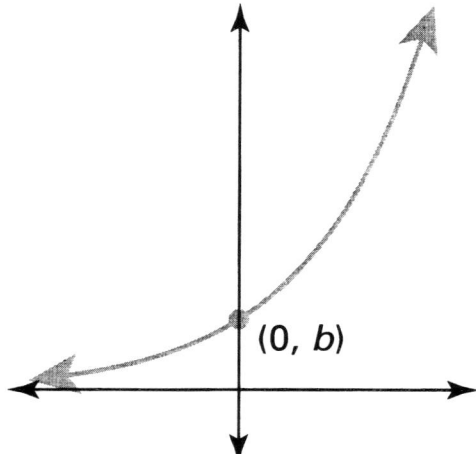

(0, *b*)

# Linear and Exponential Increase and Decrease

### Linear Increase

$y = mx + b, m > 0$

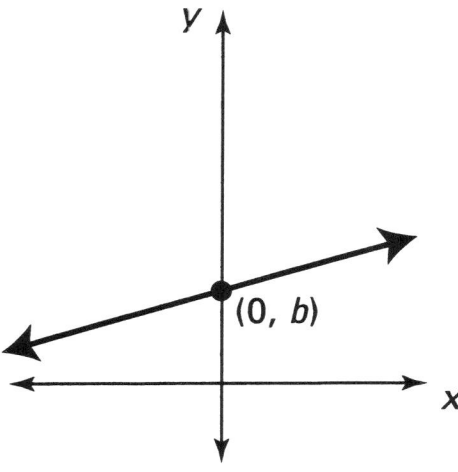

### Exponential Growth

$y = b \cdot g^x, g > 1$

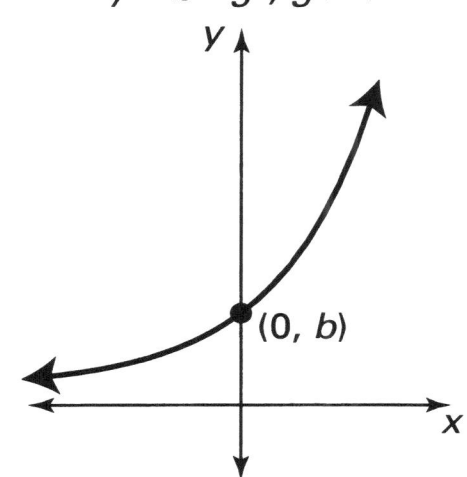

### Linear Decrease

$y = mx + b, \ m < 0$

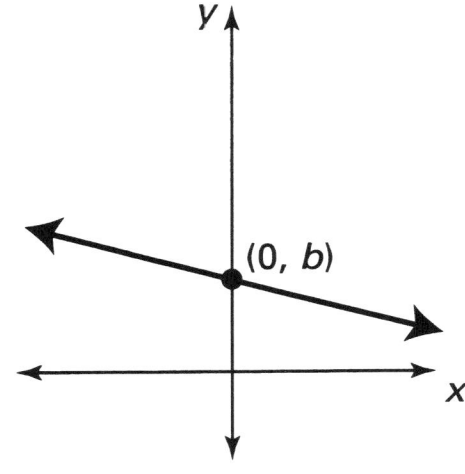

### Exponential Decay

$y = b \cdot g^x, 0 < g < 1$

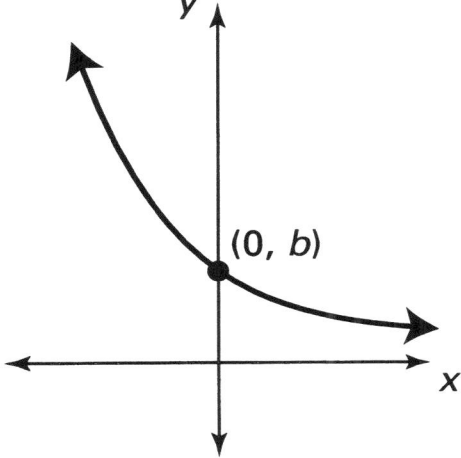

# Properties of Powers

For all exponents *m* and *n* and
nonzero bases *a* and *b:*

Zero Exponent: $b^0 = 1$

Negative Exponent: $b^{-n} = \dfrac{1}{b^n}$

Product of Powers: $b^m \cdot b^n = b^{m+n}$

Quotient of Powers: $\dfrac{b^m}{b^n} = b^{m-n}$

Power of a Power: $(b^m)^n = b^{mn}$

Power of Product: $(ab)^n = a^n b^n$

Power of a Quotient: $\left(\dfrac{a}{b}\right)^n = \dfrac{a^n}{b^n}$

## Warm-up

Lesson 9-1

1. Graph $y = -2x^2$.

2. Compare the graph you drew with the graph of $y = 2x^2$ in Example 1 on page 549. What do you notice about the graphs?

3. Compare the graph you drew with the graph shown in Example 2 on page 550. What do you notice?

## Warm-up

Lesson 9-2

Without graphing, write a short paragraph describing the graph of the equation $y = -3x^2$.

## Warm-up

Lesson 9-3

Tell what you know about *a, b,* or *c* in the equation $y = ax^2 + bx + c$ if

1. its vertex is its minimum point.

2. the *y*-axis is the axis of symmetry of the graph.

3. The point (0, 6) is on the graph.

# Warm-up

Find the coordinates of the vertex of the graph of each equation. Tell if the vertex is a minimum or a maximum.

**1.** $y = -x^2 + 4x$

**2.** $y = 6x^2$

**3.** $y = x^2 + 9$

**4.** $y = -5x^2 + 20x - 13$

# Warm-up

Evaluate each expression when $a = 4$, $b = -5$, and $c = 1$.

**1.** $-b$

**2.** $b^2 - 4ac$

**3.** $\sqrt{b^2 - 4ac}$

**4.** $-b + \sqrt{b^2 - 4ac}$

**5.** $-b - \sqrt{b^2 - 4ac}$

**6.** $\dfrac{-b + \sqrt{b^2 - 4ac}}{2a}$

**7.** $\dfrac{-b - \sqrt{b^2 - 4ac}}{2a}$

# Warm-up

**1.** Write the Quadratic Formula.

**2.** Compare what you wrote with the Quadratic Formula given on page 574. If necessary, make changes to what you wrote.

**3.** Turn your paper over and rewrite the formula from memory.

# Warm-up

**1.** Use a calculator to write the square roots of the integers from 1 to 20, truncating each answer at the thousandths place.

**2.** Which of the square roots in Question 1 are multiples of $\sqrt{2}$?

# Warm-up

In 1–6, how far is it between 0 and the given number on a number line?

**1.** 8

**2.** -8

**3.** -23

**4.** 23

**5.** $\sqrt{5}$

**6.** $-\sqrt{5}$

**7.** Graph 3, -3, $\sqrt{3}$, and $-\sqrt{3}$ on a number line.

# Warm-up

Draw a segment on a coordinate plane that is not parallel to either axis. Find the length of the segment.

# Graph of $y = x^2$

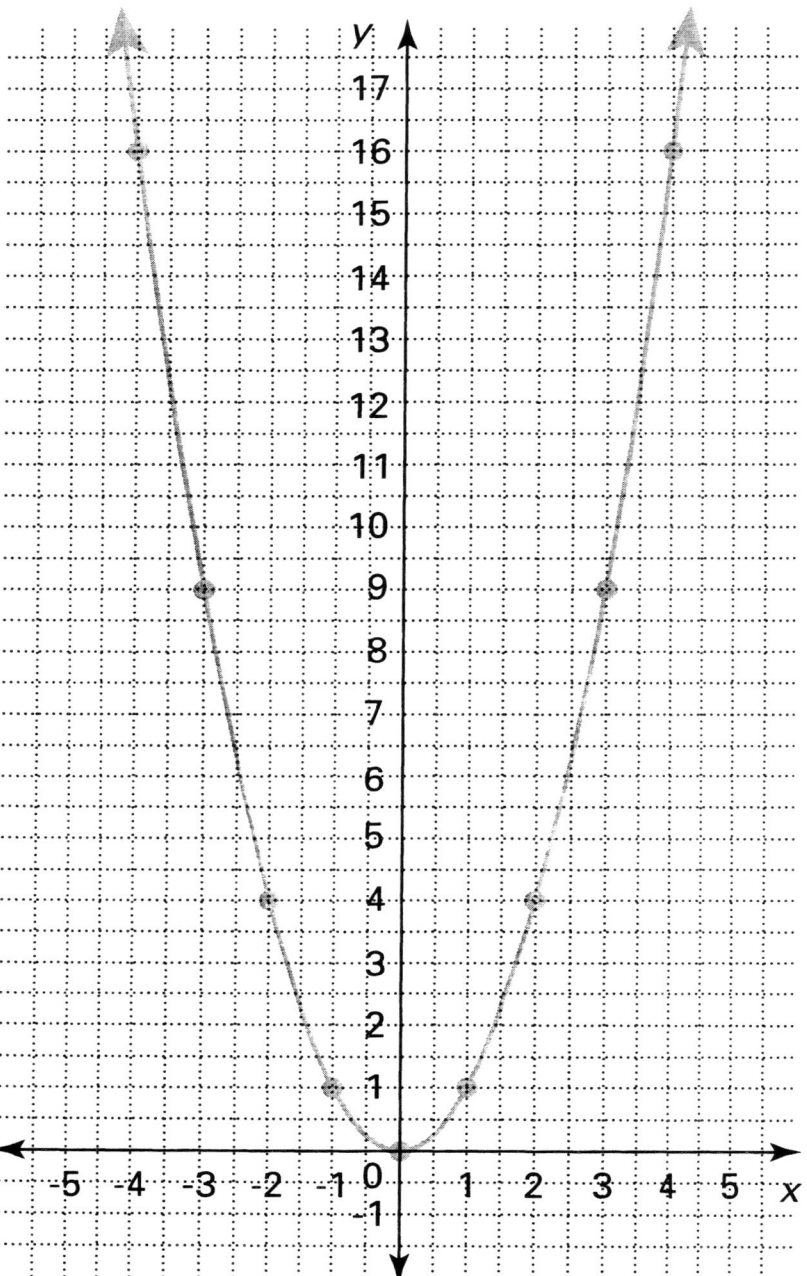

# Examples 1 and 2

## Example 1:

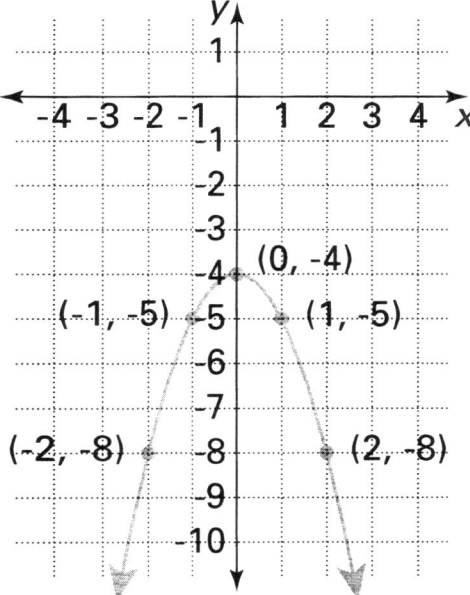

## Example 2:

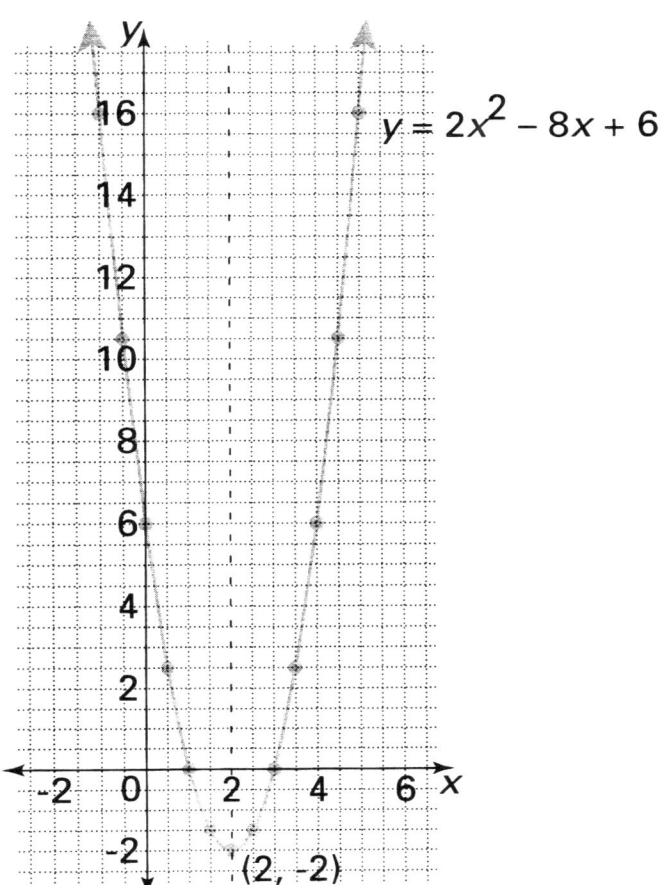

$y = 2x^2 - 8x + 6$

# Questions 12, 15–18

**12.**

| x | -8 | -7 | -6 | -5 | -4 | -3 | -2 | -1 | 0 |
|---|-----|----|----|----|----|----|----|----|---|
| y | -13 | 5  | 19 | 29 | 35 | 29 | ?  | ?  | ? |

**15.**

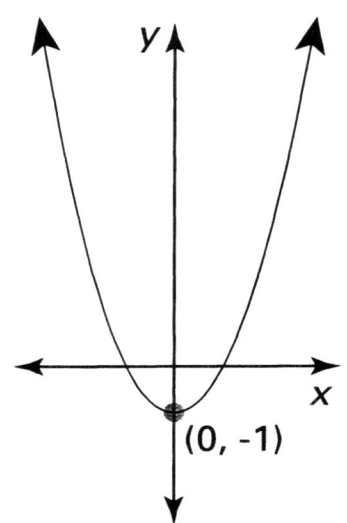

(0, -1)

**16.**

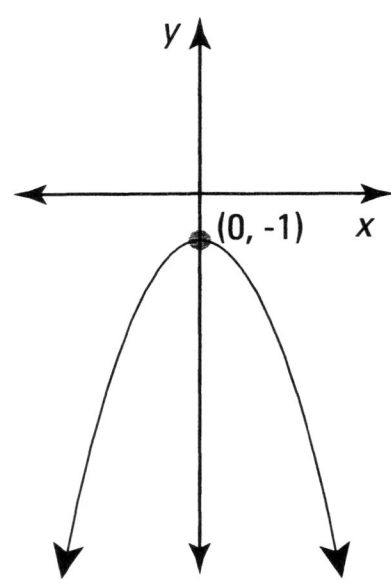

(0, -1)

**17.**

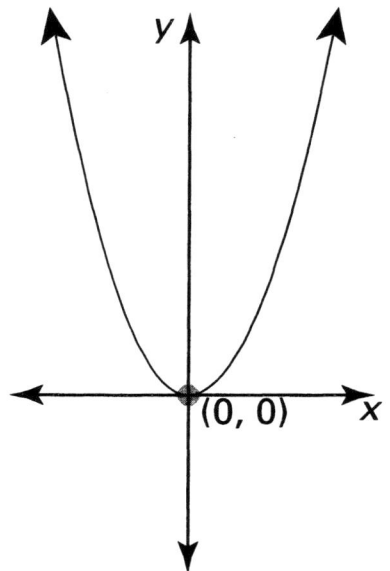

(0, 0)

**18.**

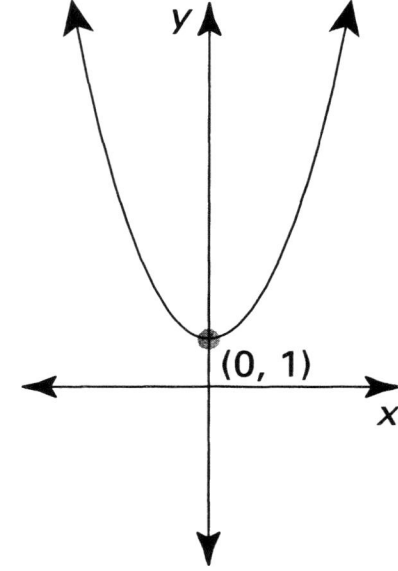

(0, 1)

# Optional Activity

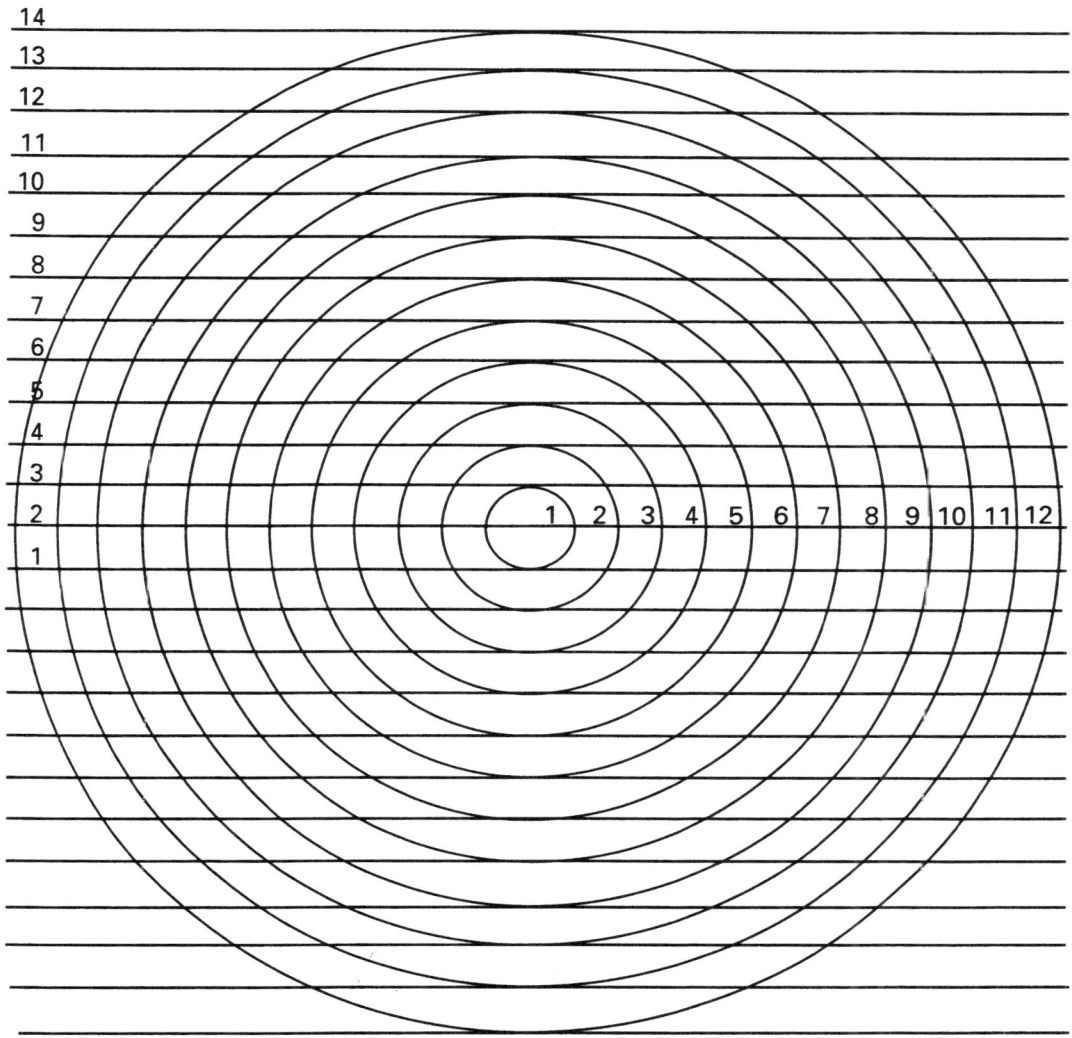

# Challenge

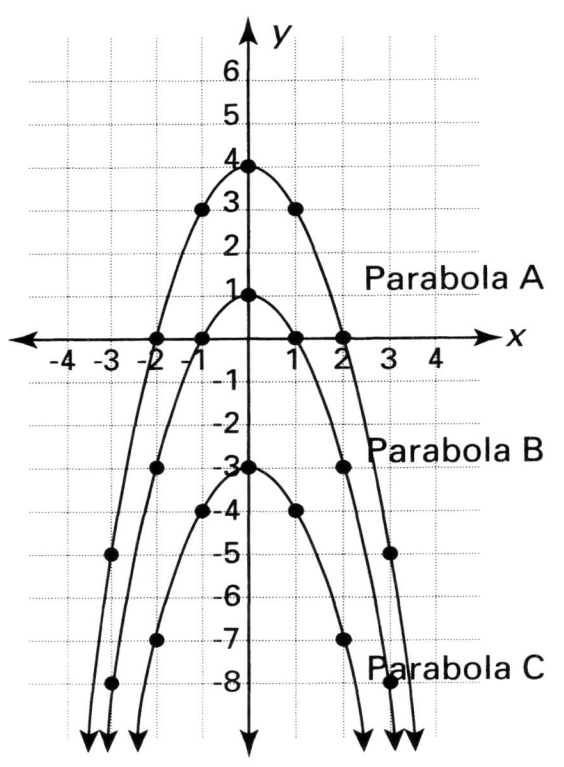 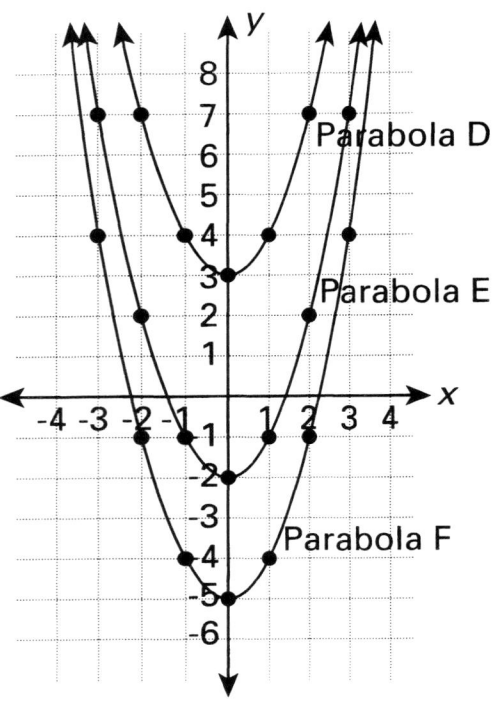

Equation A: _____

Equation B: _____

Equation C: _____

Equation D: _____

Equation E: _____

Equation F: _____

Explain how you made your decisions.

_____

_____

_____

_____

# Graphs for Examples 1 and 2

## Example 1

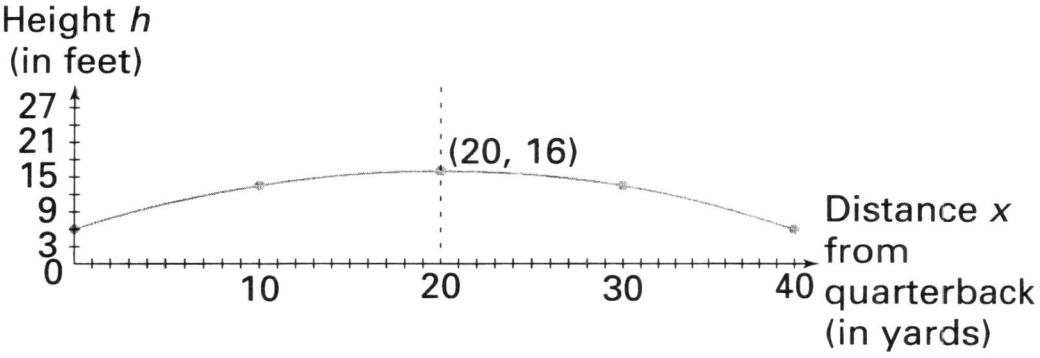

## Example 2

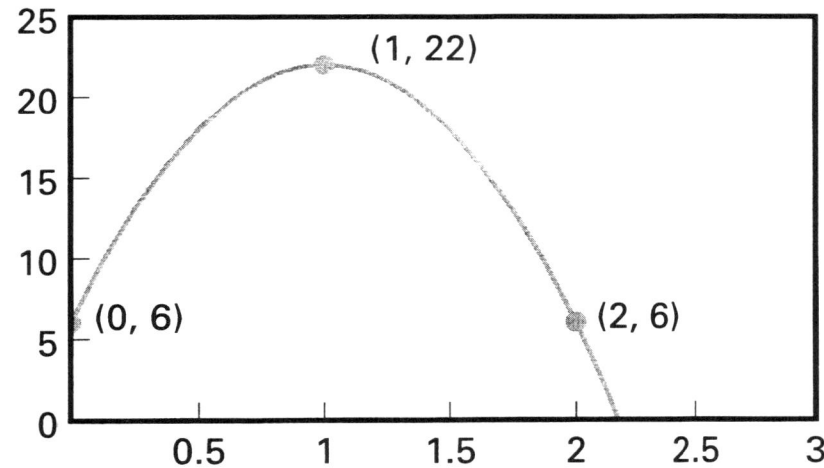

# Path of a Diver

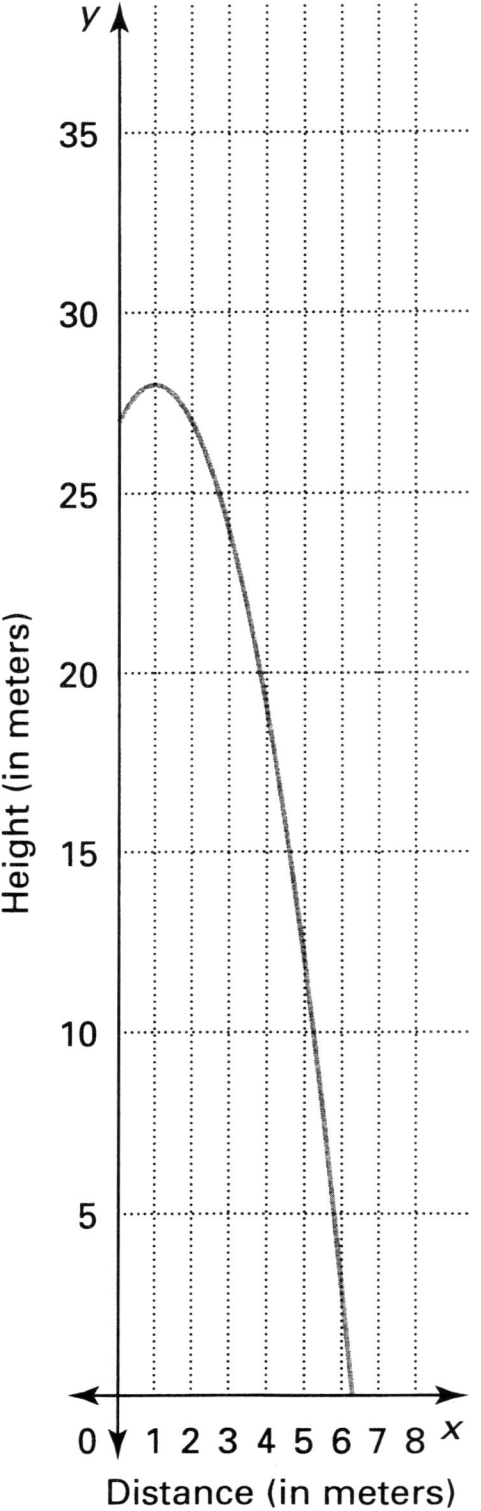

Height (in meters)

Distance (in meters)

# Additional Examples

**1.** Verify that $\sqrt{500} = 10\sqrt{5}$

    **a.** by finding decimal approximations.

    **b.** by squaring each number.

**2.** Simplify $\sqrt{150}$.

**3.** Find the exact length of the hypotenuse of this right triangle. Simplify the answer.

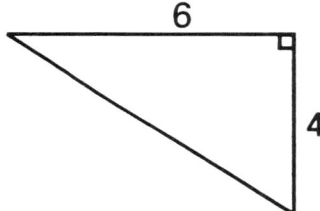

**4.** Simplify $\dfrac{-4 \pm \sqrt{48}}{8}$.

**5.** Assume $a$ and $b$ are positive. Find $\sqrt{12a} \cdot \sqrt{3b}$ and simplify the result.

**6.** Assume $a$ and $b$ are positive. Simplify $\sqrt{32a^2b^6}$.

**7.** Given that $n \geq 0$, simplify $\sqrt{11n^2}$.

**8.** Solve $y^2 + 9 = 33$ and rewrite the answer with the smallest integer possible under the radical sign.

**9.** Simplify $\sqrt{2} \cdot \sqrt{3} \cdot \sqrt{4} \cdot \sqrt{5} \cdot \sqrt{6}$.

# Additional Examples

**1.** Refer to the map on page 599. How far is it from the intersection of Divisidero and Broadway to the intersection of Franklin and Green

    **a.** traveling along Broadway and Franklin?

    **b.** as the crow flies?

**2.** Triangle *LMN* has coordinates $L = (-6, -2)$, $M = (-6, 4)$, and $N = (6, -2)$. Find *MN* as a simplified radical. Draw the triangle on a grid if necessary.

**3.** Find the distance between $(-6, 2)$ and $(-6, 7)$.

**4.** Give the distance as a simplified radical and as a decimal.

    **a.** Let $C = (4, 2)$ and $K = (7, 11)$. Find *CK*.

    **b.** Let $N = (-5, 4)$ and $Q = (2, -2)$. Find *NQ*.

**5.** Tony and Alicia each left camp on snowmobiles. Tony drove one mile north, then 5 miles west. Alicia drove 6 miles east, then 2 miles south. Make a diagram, and find the distance between Tony and Alicia.

# Warm-up

Write each number in standard form.

**1.** $3 \cdot 10^2 + 2 \cdot 10^1 + 6 \cdot 10^0$

**2.** $1 \cdot 10^3 + 4 \cdot 10^1 + 1 \cdot 10^0$

**3.** $2 \cdot 10^5 + 6 \cdot 10^3 + 8 \cdot 10^2 + 9 \cdot 10^1 + 5 \cdot 10^0$

**4.** $3 \cdot 10^5 + 6 \cdot 10^4 + 2 \cdot 10^2 + 1 \cdot 10^1$

**5.** $1 \cdot 10^6 + 8 \cdot 10^4 + 6 \cdot 10^2 + 3 \cdot 10^1 + 2 \cdot 10^0$

# Warm-up

**1.** Each of Questions 21–30 on page 626 contains at least one algebraic expression. Decide if the expression is a polynomial. If it is, tell the degree.

**2.** Name the coefficients of the terms found in Question 29 on page 626.

# Warm-up

Explain how to use the Distributive Property to shorten the work in answering each question.

**1.** Kate, Anne, Laura, and Michael each bought a concert ticket for $32, a program for $10, and a shirt for $18. How much did they spend altogether?

**2.** Mr. Enge bought 6 pairs of socks for $1.79 a pair and 6 cans of tennis balls for $2.29 per can. What was the total cost?

## Warm-up

Multiply.

**1.** $3x(x + 7)$           **2.** $2(5x - 3)$

**3.** $8x^2(2x + 3y + 4)$        **4.** $10y(x^3 - x + y)$

**5.** $6x(6x - 6)$         **6.** $x^2(2x^2 + xy - 4y^2)$

## Warm-up

Write each expression as a trinomial.

**1.** $2y^2 + 3y - 4y - 21$     **2.** $24x^2 + 30x + 4x + 5$

**3.** $5y^2 + 5xy - xy - x^2$     **4.** $18x^2 - 27xy + 8yx - 12y^2$

**5.** $3t \cdot 3t + 7 \cdot 3t + 7 \cdot 3t + 7 \cdot 7$

**6.** $2y \cdot 2y + 2y \cdot 5 + 3 \cdot 2y + 3 \cdot 5$

## Warm-up

**1. a.** Multiply $50 + 7$ by $30 + 3$ by thinking of $50 + 7$ and $30 + 3$ as binomials.

    **b.** Does the process give the answer to $57 \cdot 33$? If so, show that it does.

**2.** Use the same process described in Question 1a to explain how to multiply $32 \cdot 61$ mentally.

# Warm-up

Solve the following problems.

**1.** If a spinner is divided into four congruent regions that are numbered 1, 2, 3, and 4, and you spin it 120 times, how many times would you expect the spinner to land on 2?

**2.** If you randomly asked 70 people on what day of the week their birthday falls this year, how many would you expect to say Tuesday?

**3.** If you randomly asked 100 people if their home telephone number ended in an even or an odd number, how many would you expect to say odd?

**4.** If you tossed a die 90 times, how many times would you expect to toss a 3?

# Classifying Polynomials

| Degree | Name of Polynomial |
|--------|--------------------|
| 1 | linear |
| 2 | quadratic |
| 3 | cubic |
| 4 | quartic |
| 5 | quintic |
| 6 | no special name |

| Number of Terms | Name of Polynomial |
|-----------------|--------------------|
| 1 | monomial |
| 2 | binomial |
| 3 | trinomial |
| 4 | no special name |
| 5 | no special name |
| 6 | no special name |

# Challenge

| A | |
|---|---|
| 1 | 9 |
| 3 | 11 |
| 5 | 13 |
| 7 | 15 |

| B | |
|---|---|
| 2 | 10 |
| 3 | 11 |
| 6 | 14 |
| 7 | 15 |

| C | |
|---|---|
| 4 | 12 |
| 5 | 13 |
| 6 | 14 |
| 7 | 15 |

| D | |
|---|---|
| 8 | 12 |
| 9 | 13 |
| 10 | 14 |
| 11 | 15 |

# Example 3

| | A | B | C | D | E |
|---|---|---|---|---|---|
| | | | | | |
| 1 | Year | Nellie's Deposit | Nellie's Balance | Joe's Deposit | Joe's Balance |
| 2 | | | (end of year) | | (end of year) |
| 3 | 1 | 1000 | 1060.00 | 0 | 0 |
| 4 | 2 | 1000 | 2183.60 | 0 | 0 |
| 5 | 3 | 1000 | 3374.62 | 0 | 0 |
| 6 | 4 | 1000 | 4637.09 | 0 | 0 |
| 7 | 5 | 1000 | 5975.32 | 0 | 0 |
| 8 | 6 | 0 | 6333.84 | 1200 | 1272.00 |
| 9 | 7 | 0 | 6713.87 | 1200 | 2620.32 |
| 10 | 8 | 0 | 7116.70 | 1200 | 4049.54 |
| 11 | 9 | 0 | 7543.70 | 1200 | 5564.51 |
| 12 | 10 | 0 | 7996.32 | 1200 | 7170.38 |

# Extension

## Polynomials from Mortgage Payments

Starting amount of mortgage: $50,000    Annual interest rate: 10%

Monthly payment for principal
and interest:    $  439    Monthly interest rate: $\frac{10\%}{12} = .0083$

| Month | Amount owed ($) | |
|---|---|---|
| 0 | 50,000 | = 50,000.00 |
| 1 | 50,000(1.0083) − 439 | = 49,976.00 |
| 2 | [50,000(1.0083) − 439](1.0083) − 439 or | |
| | 50,000(1.0083)$^2$ − 439(1.0083) − 439 | = 49,951.80 |
| 3 | [50,000(1.0083)$^2$ − 439(1.0083) − 439](1.0083) − 439 or | |
| | 50,000(1.0083)$^3$ − 439(1.0083)$^2$ − 439(1.0083) − 439 | = 49,927.40 |
| 4 | 50,000(1.0083)$^4$ − 439(1.0083)$^3$ − 439(1.0083)$^2$ − 439(1.0083) − 439 | = 49,902.80 |
| 5 | | |
| 6 | | |

## Example 1

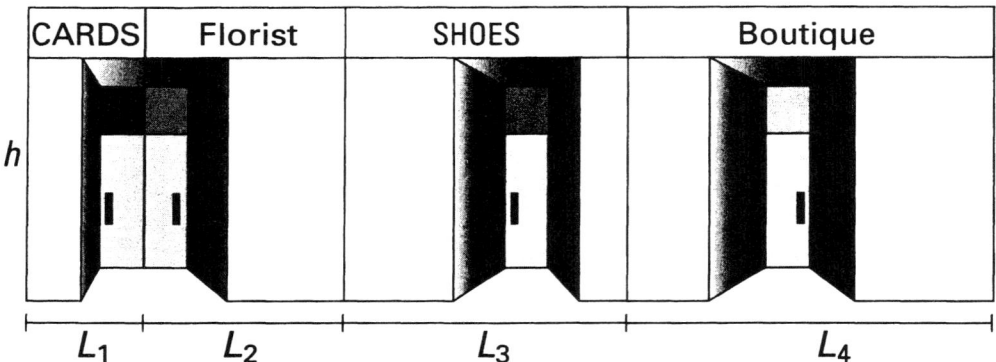

CARDS | Florist | SHOES | Boutique

$h$

$L_1$  $L_2$  $L_3$  $L_4$

---

## Additional Examples

**1.** Give two equivalent expressions for the area pictured below.

| | $x$ | $x$ | $x$ | $x$ |
|---|---|---|---|---|
| $x$ | $x^2$ | $x^2$ | $x^2$ | $x^2$ |
| $x$ | $x^2$ | $x^2$ | $x^2$ | $x^2$ |
| 1 | $x$ | $x$ | $x$ | $x$ |
| 1 | $x$ | $x$ | $x$ | $x$ |
| 1 | $x$ | $x$ | $x$ | $x$ |
| 1 | $x$ | $x$ | $x$ | $x$ |

**2.** Multiply $-5y(y^3 - 6y^2 + 2y + 6)$.

**3.** Multiply $k^4(k^2 - 16km)$.

# Multiplying Polynomials

| | a | b | c | d |
|---|---|---|---|---|
| x | ax | bx | cx | dx |
| y | ay | by | cy | dy |
| z | az | bz | cz | dz |

# Questions 1 and 9

**1.**

|  | $w^2$ | $5w$ | 4 |
|---|---|---|---|
| $w$ |  |  |  |
| 6 |  |  |  |

**9.**

|  | $x$ | $y$ | 5 |
|---|---|---|---|
| $x$ |  |  |  |
| $y$ |  |  |  |
| 2 |  |  |  |

# Questions 1, 2, 13, and 14

**1.**

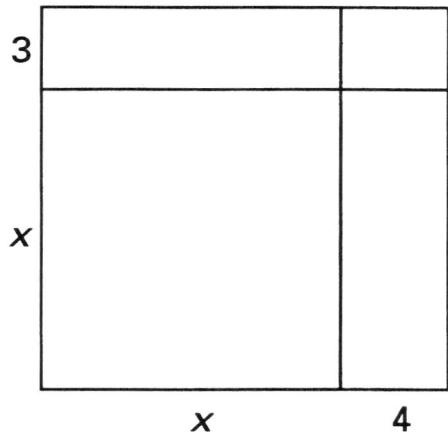

**2.**

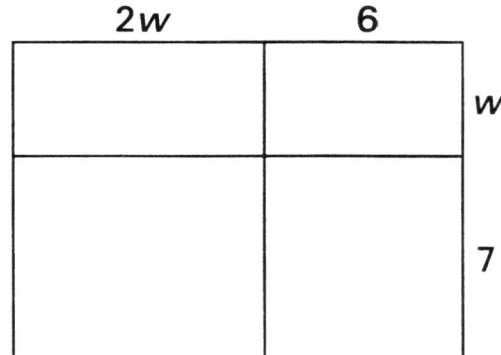

**13.**

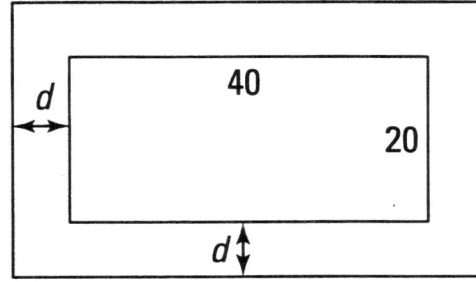

**14.**

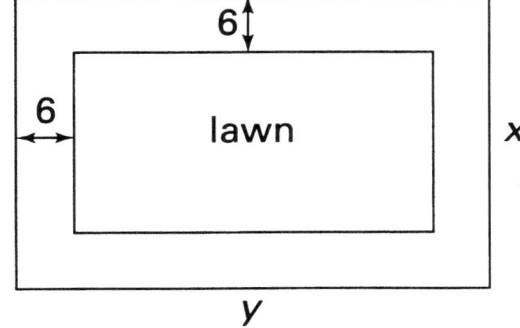

# Special Binomial Products

## The Square of a Sum

## The Square of a Difference

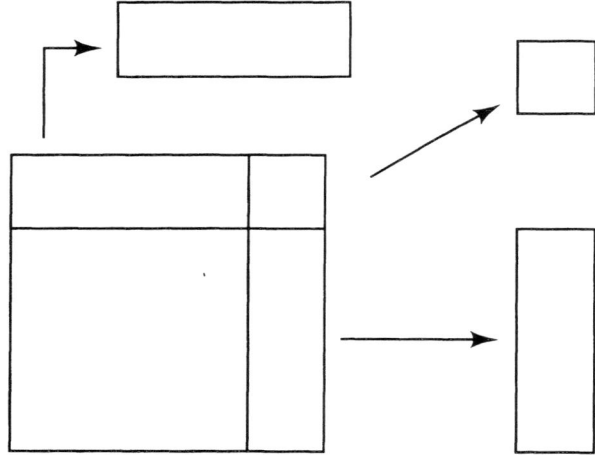

## The Difference of Two Squares

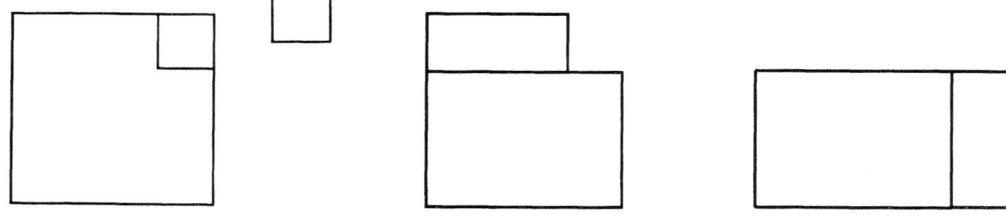

# Critical Chi-Square Values

| $n-1$ | .10 | .05 | .01 | .001 |
|---|---|---|---|---|
| 1 | 2.71 | 3.84 | 6.63 | 10.8 |
| 2 | 4.61 | 5.99 | 9.21 | 13.8 |
| 3 | 6.25 | 7.81 | 11.34 | 16.3 |
| 4 | 7.78 | 9.49 | 13.28 | 18.5 |
| 5 | 9.24 | 11.07 | 15.09 | 20.5 |
| 6 | 10.6 | 12.6 | 16.8 | 22.5 |
| 7 | 12.0 | 14.1 | 18.5 | 24.3 |
| 8 | 13.4 | 15.5 | 20.1 | 26.1 |
| 9 | 14.7 | 16.9 | 21.7 | 27.9 |
| 10 | 16.0 | 18.3 | 23.2 | 29.6 |
| 11 | 17.3 | 19.7 | 24.7 | 31.3 |
| 12 | 18.6 | 21.0 | 26.2 | 32.9 |
| 13 | 19.8 | 22.4 | 27.7 | 34.5 |
| 14 | 21.1 | 23.7 | 29.1 | 36.1 |
| 15 | 22.3 | 25.0 | 30.6 | 37.7 |
| 16 | 23.5 | 26.3 | 32.0 | 39.3 |
| 17 | 24.8 | 27.6 | 33.4 | 40.8 |
| 18 | 26.0 | 28.9 | 34.8 | 42.3 |
| 19 | 27.2 | 30.1 | 36.2 | 43.8 |
| 20 | 28.4 | 31.4 | 37.6 | 45.3 |
| 25 | 34.4 | 37.7 | 44.3 | 52.6 |
| 30 | 40.3 | 43.8 | 50.9 | 59.7 |
| 50 | 63.2 | 67.5 | 76.2 | 86.7 |

# Additional Examples

One die was tossed 60 times to see if it was fair. Here are the results of the tosses: 26225 23635 12224 12154 55351 42545 66465 46522 13224 23645 35552 44423.

**1.** What are the observed values for the events of getting a 1, 2, 3, 4, 5, and 6 in this situation?

**2.** What are the expected values of each event?

**3.** Use the chi-square statistic to give some evidence whether or not the die is fair.

# Warm-up

**1.** Find the single pair of numbers $x$ and $y$ that satisfy both of the equations: $x + y = 10$ and $x - y = 4$.

In 2–5, find a solution for each pair of equations. Use any method that works for you.

**2.** $x + y = 95$ and $x - y = 37$

**3.** $a + b = 100$ and $a - b = 25$

**4.** $p + q = 1$ and $p - q = \frac{3}{5}$

**5.** $m + n = -7$ and $m - n = 2$

# Warm-up

Bank A charges a $3 monthly fee for a checking account and 10¢ for each check that is written. Bank B charges a $5 monthly fee, but no additional fee for each check that is written. When is it less expensive to have a checking account at Bank A? How did you arrive at your answer?

# Warm-up

For each question tell which, if any, of the equations are equivalent.

**1. a.** $x - y = 65$

   **b.** $x = 65 + y$

   **c.** $y = x + 65$

**2. a.** $2x + y = 10$

   **b.** $y = 2x - 10$

   **c.** $y = 10 + 2x$

**3. a.** $y = \frac{x + 6}{4}$

   **b.** $x = 4y - 6$

   **c.** $4y = x + 6$

**4. a.** $2x + y = 4$

   **b.** $y = \frac{12 + 6x}{3}$

   **c.** $6x + 3y = 12$

# Warm-up

A large cheese pizza with one additional topping costs $8.99. A large cheese pizza with three additional toppings costs $11.29. Assuming each topping costs the same amount, find the price of each topping and the price of a large cheese pizza with no additional topping.

# Warm-up

Define each form or property.

**1.** Standard form of an equation

**2.** Slope-intercept form of an equation

**3.** Generalized Addition Property of Equality

**4.** Multiplication Property of Equality

# Warm-up

Write each equation in slope-intercept form.

**1.** $-6x + y = -2$

**2.** $15x + 5y = -10$

**3.** $-5x + y = -3$

**4.** $2y - 20x = 0$

**5.** $3y - 18x = 3$

**6.** If the equations in Questions 1–5 were graphed, which equations, if any, would result in parallel lines?

# Warm-up

Describe three situations that are always true and three situations that are never true.

# Warm-up

Write a paragraph that explains how to graph the inequality $y > \frac{1}{2}x - 3$.

# Olympic 100-Meter Freestyle

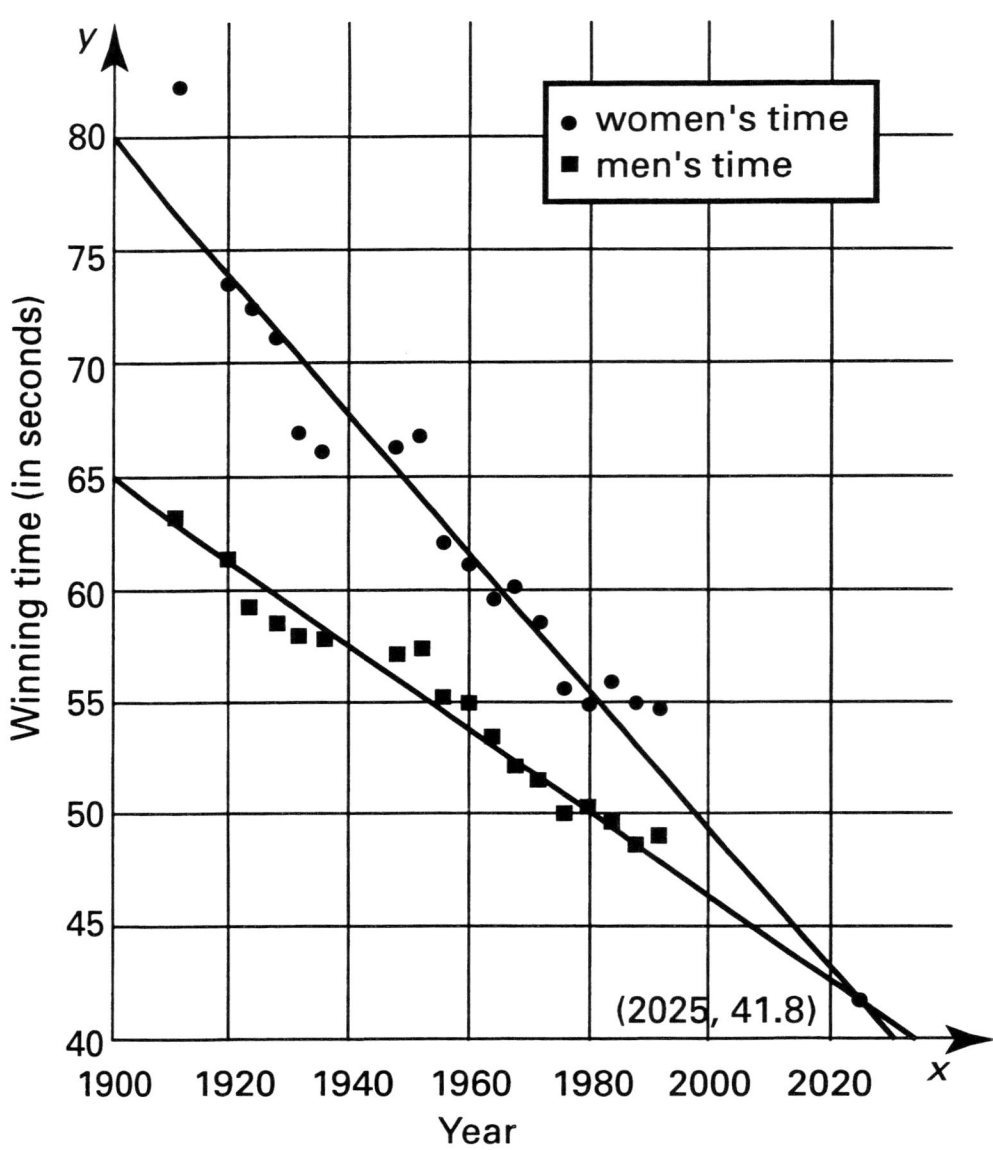

# Four Ways to Write the Solution to a System

| There are four ways to write the solution to a system of equations with two variables: | The solution to $\begin{cases} x + y = 22 \\ x - y = 8 \end{cases}$ can be written as: |
|---|---|
| (1) as an ordered pair | $(15, 7)$ |
| (2) as an ordered pair identifying the variables | $(x, y) = (15, 7)$ |
| (3) by naming the variables individually | $x = 15$ and $y = 7$ |
| (4) as a set of ordered pairs | $\{(15, 7)\}$ |

## Additional Examples

**1.** Going with the wind, a blimp flies 360 miles to an air show. The trip takes 4 hours. The return trip, flying against the wind, takes 9 hours. How fast is the blimp flying in still air? What is the speed of the wind?

**2.** Solve this system.
$$\begin{cases} 2x - 5y = 18 \\ 4x - 5y = -4 \end{cases}$$

**3.** At the 1987 annual meeting of the National Council of Teachers of Mathematics, the system below was found on a menu card at a restaurant in California. (Yes, the system really did appear on the bottom of the menu card.) How much did each item in column A cost, and how much did each item in column B cost?

| *Multiple Choice* |
| --- |
| *2 or more entrées* |
| Choose 1 from column A and |
| 1 from column B — $5.49 |
| Choose 1 from column A and |
| 2 from column B — $6.99 |

| **A** | **B** |
| --- | --- |
| • Chicken Dijon | • Fried Chicken |
| • Top Sirloin Steak | (2 pieces) |
| • Steak Dijon | • Battered Cod |
| • Fried Chicken | • Shrimp |
| | • Chicken Strips |

A + B = $5.49

A + 2B = $6.99

# Warm-up

Work in a group.

**1.** Each of you think of a number greater than 100 and less than 1000 that is not prime. Give the number to the other members of your group.

**2.** Factor all the numbers from the other members of your group.

# Warm-up

Answer each question by using prime factorization.

**1.** What are the factors of 200?

**2.** Find the greatest common factor of 288 and 12.

**3.** Find the greatest common factor of 72 and 128.

**4.** What are the factors of $n^2$?

**5.** Find the greatest common factor of $n^5$ and $n^3$.

**6.** What is the greatest common factor of $x^2n$, $xn^2t$, and $xnt^2$?

# Warm-up

Find two numbers whose product is the first number and whose sum is the second number.

**1.** 96; 28

**2.** 90; -21

**3.** -165; 28

**4.** -153; -8

# Warm-up

When will the quadratic equation, $ax^2 + bx + c = 0$ have

**1.** exactly two real solutions?

**2.** exactly one real solution?

**3.** no real solutions?

**4.** What property can be used to answer Questions 1–3?

# Warm-up

Tell whether or not each polynomial is factorable. If the polynomial is factorable, factor it.

**1.** $x^2 - 6x - 3$

**2.** $x^2 + 2x - 8$

**3.** $x^2 - 81$

**4.** $x^2 + 13x + 42$

**5.** $x^2 - 13x + 40$

**6.** $x^2 + 13x + 25$

# Warm-up

Use the Quadratic Formula to solve
each equation.

**1.** $m^2 - 21m + 108 = 0$    **2.** $12x^2 + 7x = 10$

# Warm-up

Write each number as a fraction.

**1.** 0.75    **2.** $2\frac{3}{8}$

**3.** $0.\overline{6}$    **4.** 4.65

**5.** 6.092    **6.** 26%

# Warm-up

Tell how many real solutions each
quadratic equation has.

**1.** $x^2 - 6x + 9 = 0$

**2.** $4x^2 + x + 7 = 0$

**3.** $2x^2 - 5x - 1 = 0$

**4.** $x^2 + 2x + 3 = 0$

**5.** $3x^2 - 7x + 2 = 0$

**6.** $x^2 - 16 = 0$

# Question 32

| Diameter (in.) | Volume (ft³) | Diameter (in.) | Volume (ft³) |
| --- | --- | --- | --- |
| 8.3 | 10.3 | 12.9 | 33.8 |
| 8.6 | 10.3 | 13.3 | 27.4 |
| 8.8 | 10.2 | 13.7 | 25.7 |
| 10.5 | 16.4 | 13.8 | 24.7 |
| 10.7 | 18.8 | 14.0 | 34.5 |
| 11.0 | 15.6 | 14.2 | 31.7 |
| 11.0 | 18.2 | 14.5 | 36.3 |
| 11.1 | 22.6 | 16.3 | 42.6 |
| 11.2 | 19.9 | 17.3 | 55.4 |
| 11.3 | 24.2 | 17.5 | 55.7 |
| 11.4 | 21.0 | 17.9 | 58.3 |
| 11.4 | 21.4 | 18.0 | 51.0 |
| 11.7 | 21.3 | 18.0 | 51.5 |
| 12.0 | 19.1 | 20.6 | 77.0 |
| 12.9 | 22.2 | | |

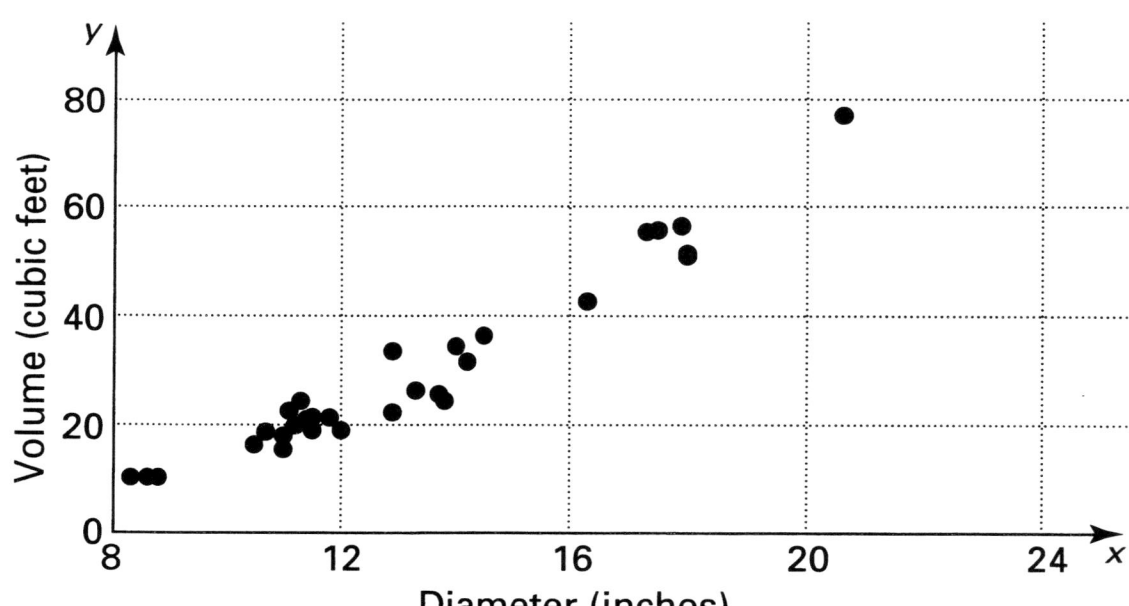

Diameter (inches)
4.5 ft above ground level

# Warm-up

1. As a class, make a list of the different shapes of graphs you have studied this year.

2. Work with a partner. For each graph on the class list, write an equation that gives that kind of graph. Also give a few values that satisfy the equation.

# Warm-up

Find the values of $y$ when $x = 1$, -2, 6, and 0.

**1.** $y = -2x$     **2.** $y = 50 - 5x$     **3.** $y = x^2 + 4$

**4.** $y = 100 + .5x$     **5.** $y = 2^x$     **6.** $y = 2x^2 + x - 3$

# Warm-up

A baseball is supposed to weigh 5.125 ounces with an allowable weight tolerance of ±0.125 ounce.

1. What is the least amount a baseball can weigh?

2. What is the greatest amount a baseball can weigh?

3. If $b$ is the weight of a baseball that falls within the allowable weight tolerance, what is true about $|b - 5.125|$?

# Warm-up

Find three ordered pairs for each function.

**1.** $f(x) = x^2 + 1$          **2.** $g(x) = 7$

**3.** $h(x) = 2x$          **4.** $p(x) = x^2 + 2x + 2$

# Warm-up

Suppose there are 26 pieces of paper in a dish. Each paper has a different letter of the alphabet written on it. Determine the probability of

**1.** picking the letter Z.

**2.** picking the letter A.

**3.** picking a letter that comes before N in the alphabet.

**4.** picking one of the letters of ALGEBRA.

# Warm-up

**1.** Sketch the graphs of $y = x$ and $y = x^3$ on the same grid.

**2.** Sketch the graphs of $y = x^2$ and $y = x^4$ on the same grid.

**3.** In which quadrants will the graph of $y = x^5$ fall? Why?

**4.** In which quadrants will the graph of $y = x^6$ fall? Why?

# Warm-up

**1.** Measure the sides of △ABC in millimeters.

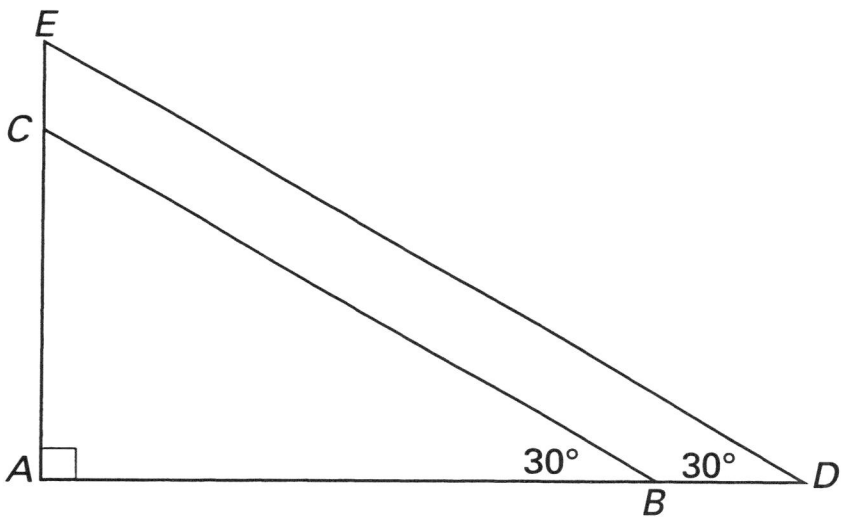

**2.** In △*ABC* find the ratio of these measures.

$$\frac{\text{leg opposite the 30° angle}}{\text{leg adjacent to the 30° angle}}$$

**3.** Repeat Questions 1–2 for △*ADE*.

**4.** Find the tangent of 30° on your calculator. Compare it with the ratios you found for △*ABC* and △*ADE*.

# Warm-up

Make a list of at least 5 keys on your calculator that you have used this year other than the number keys or basic operation keys. Give an example of how each key is used.

# Functions

## Value of Investment at 6% Annual Yield

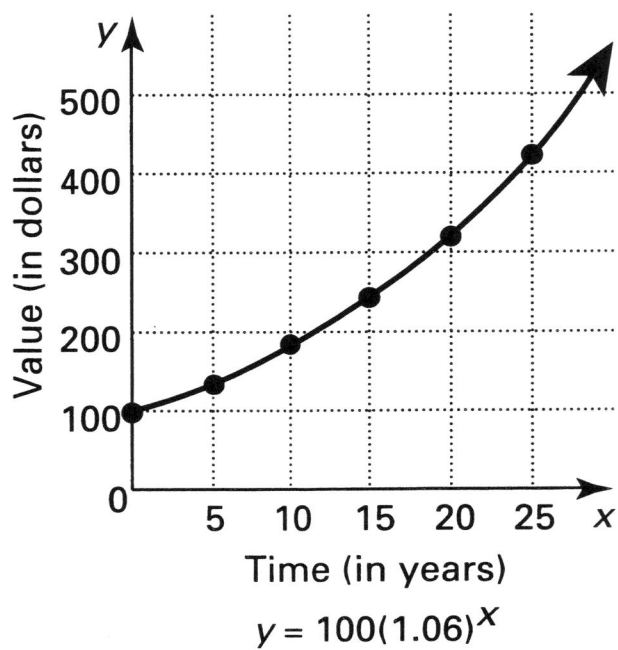

$y = 100(1.06)^x$

## Fahrenheit-Celsius Temperatures

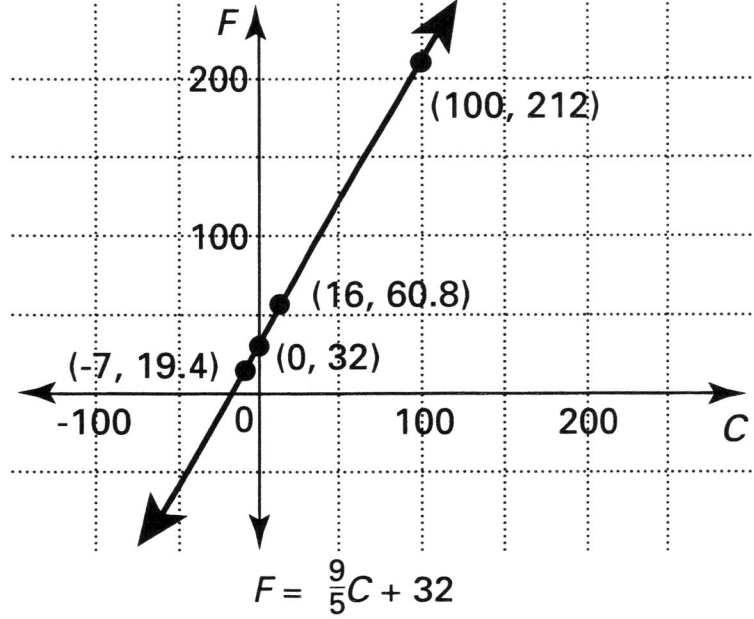

$F = \frac{9}{5}C + 32$

# Additional Examples

**1.** Does $x = y^2 - 3y + 2$ describe a function? Why or why not?

**2.** The chart describes the severity of hurricanes.

| Category | Sustained Winds (mph) | Damage |
|---|---|---|
| 1 | 74-95 | Minimal |
| 2 | 96-110 | Moderate |
| 3 | 111-130 | Extensive |
| 4 | 131-155 | Extreme |
| 5 | 156 or more | Catastrophic |

Does the set of ordered pairs describe a function? Explain.

**a.** (category, wind speed)

**b.** (wind speed, damage)

**c.** (damage, category)

## Test-Flight Graph

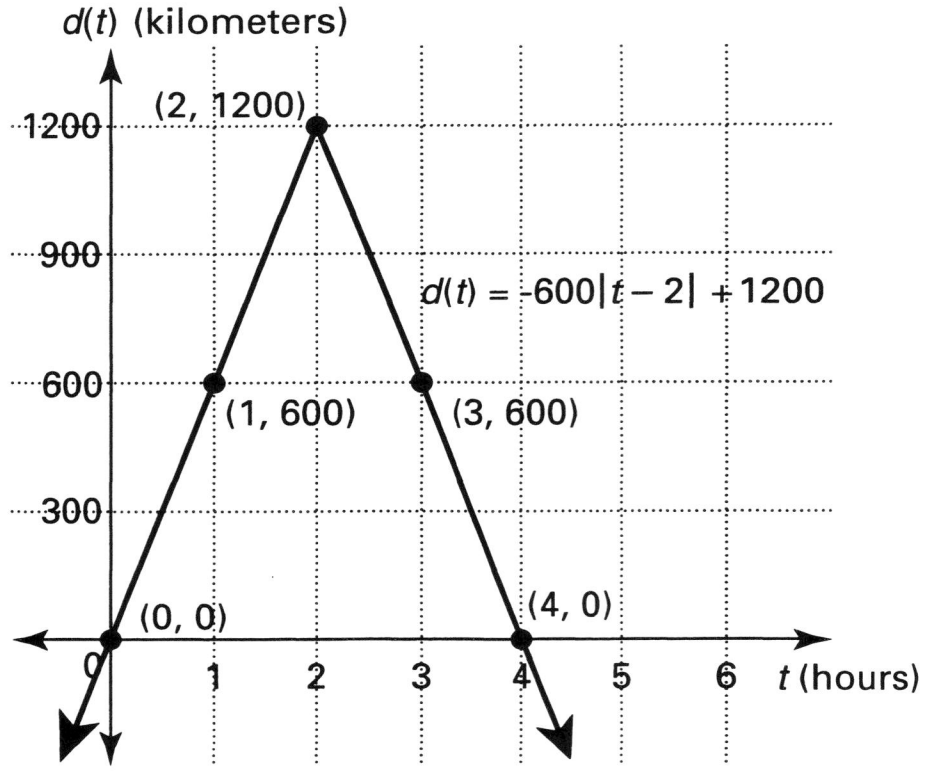

$d(t)$ (kilometers)

(2, 1200)

1200

900

$d(t) = -600|t - 2| + 1200$

600

(1, 600)    (3, 600)

300

(0, 0)    (4, 0)

0    1    2    3    4    5    6    $t$ (hours)

## Questions 16–17

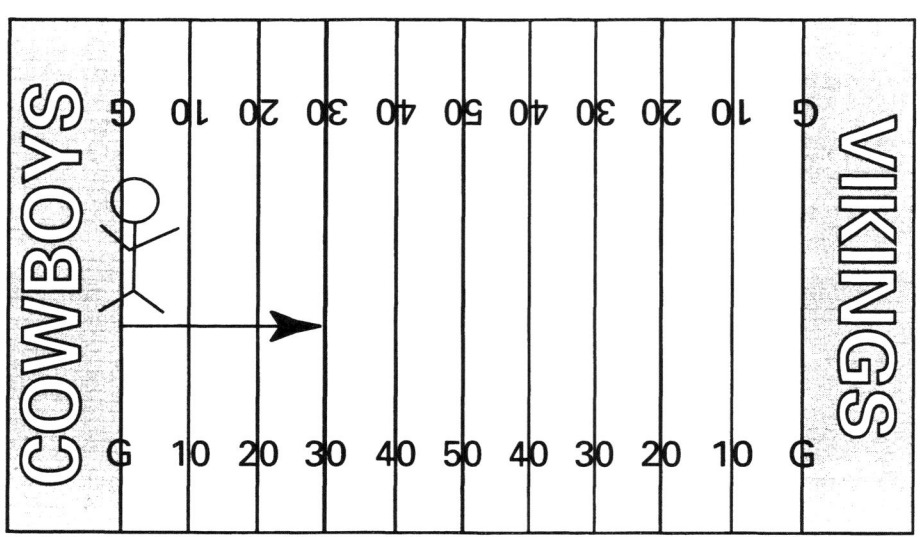

# Domain and Range

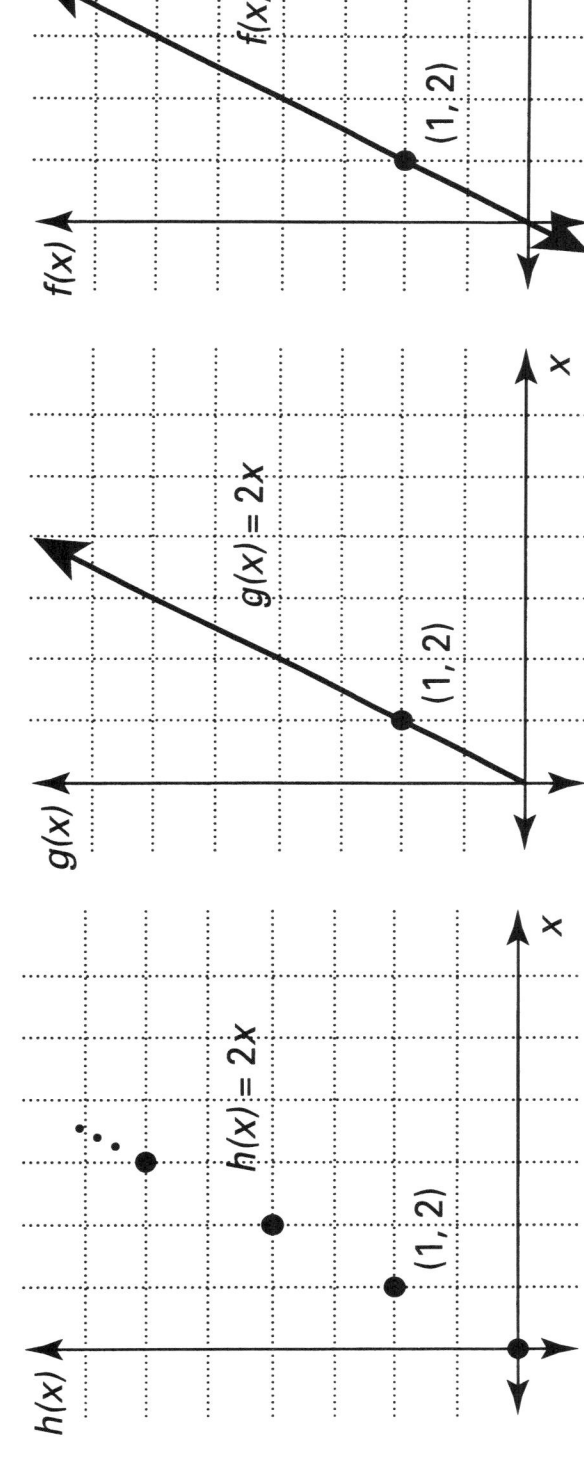

### h(x)

h(x) = 2x

(1, 2)

x

domain = set of
nonnegative
integers

range = set of
nonnegative
even integers

### g(x)

g(x) = 2x

(1, 2)

x

domain = set of all
nonnegative
real numbers

range = set of
nonnegative
real numbers

### f(x)

f(x) = 2x

(1, 2)

x

domain = set of all real
numbers

range = set of all real
numbers

# Additional Examples

**1.** Assume that it is equally likely that the spinner below lands on each position.

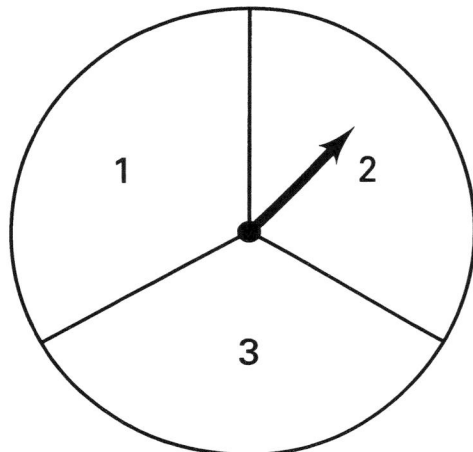

    **a.** Let $P(n)$ = the probability of landing in region $n$. Graph the function $P$.

    **b.** Give an equation for the function.

**2.** Assume that four fair coins are tossed. Let $P(t)$ = the probability of tossing $t$ tails. Give the ordered pairs of this function. Hint: First make a list of all possible outcomes.

# Examples 1–3

**1.**

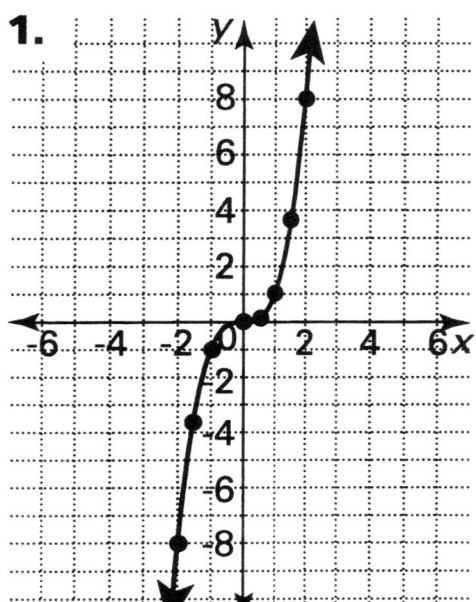

**2.**

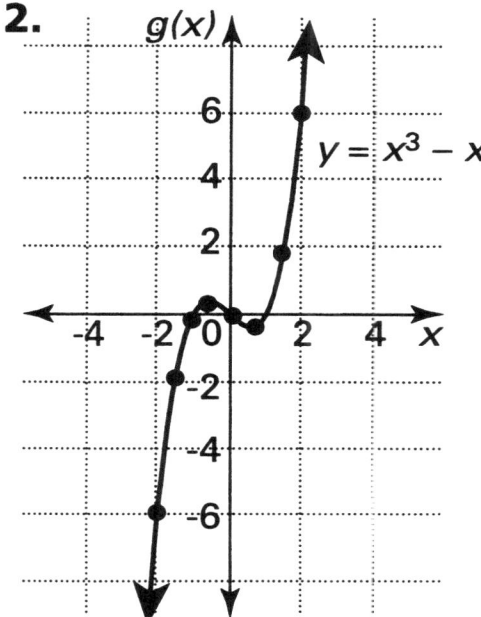

$y = x^3 - x$

**3.**

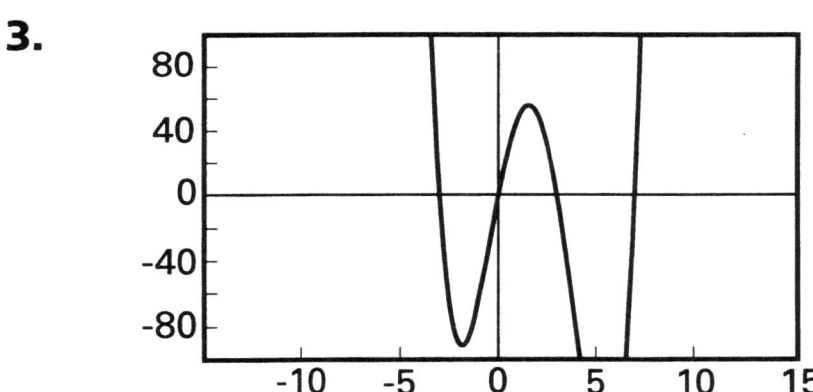

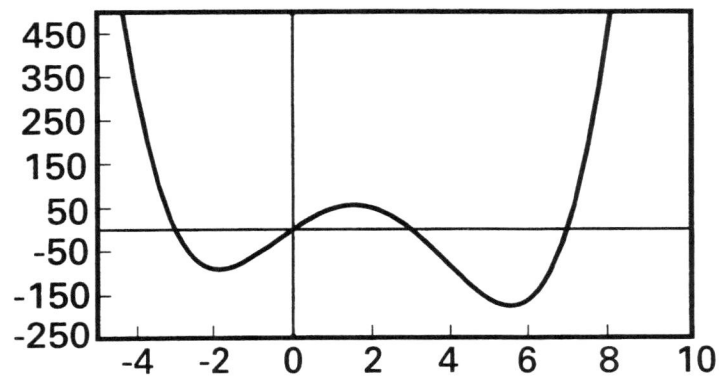

## Activity

| x | tan x |
|-----|-------|
| 10° | 0.176 |
| 20° | 0.364 |
| 30° | 0.577 |
| 40° | 0.839 |
| 50° | 1.192 |
| 60° | 1.732 |
| 70° | 2.747 |
| 80° | 5.671 |

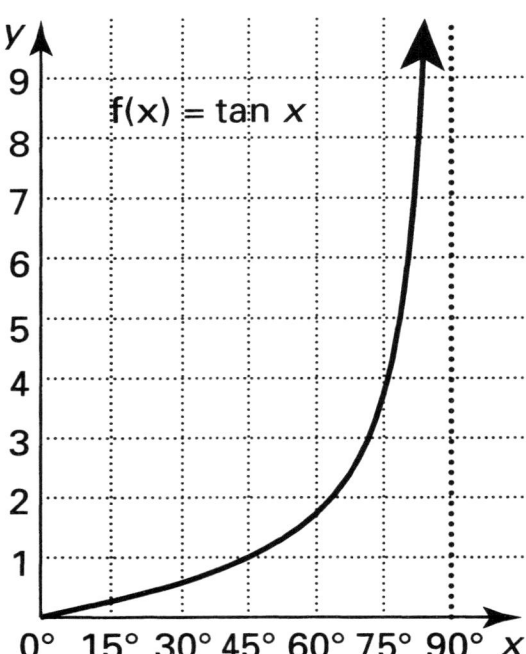

## Example

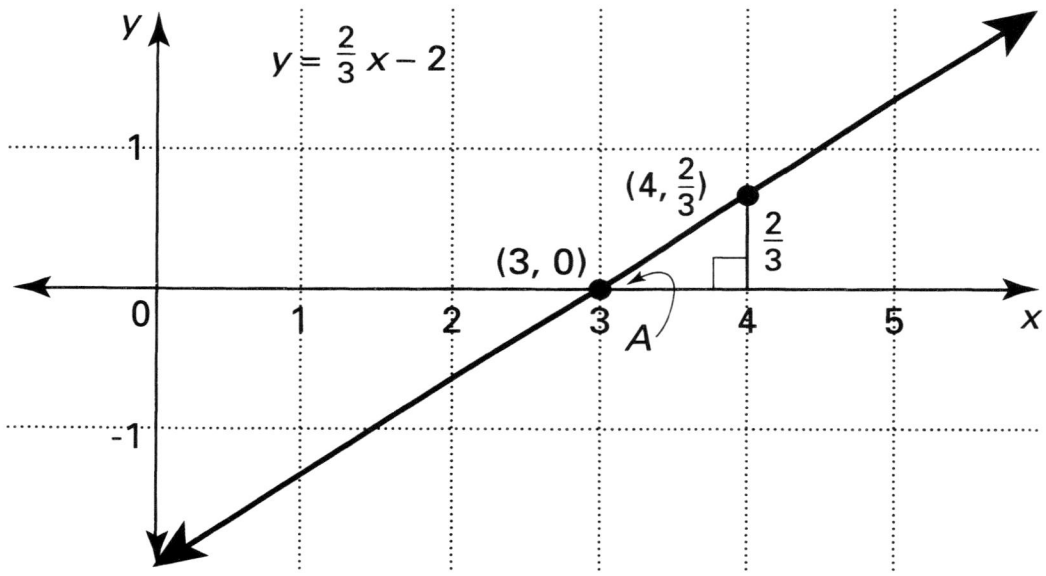

# Additional Examples

**1.** In △*PQR*, find tan *P*.

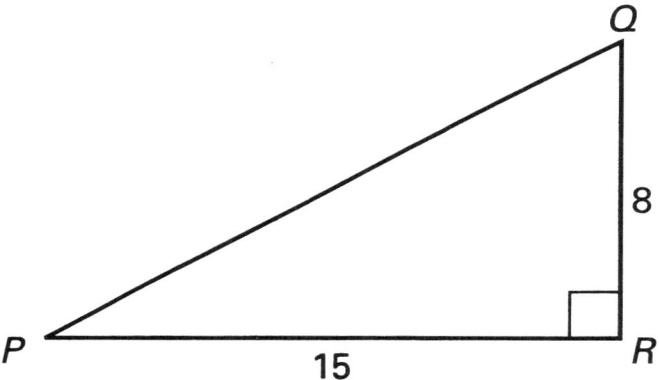

**2.** When Betsy and her brother Bob are standing 4 feet apart, Betsy must look up at an angle of 36° to see the top of his head. If her eyes are 40 inches above the ground, about how tall is Bob?

**3.** Suppose an airplane takes off at a 15° angle. After it has traveled 600 feet horizontally, how far is the plane above the ground?

# Graphs of y = sin x and y = log x

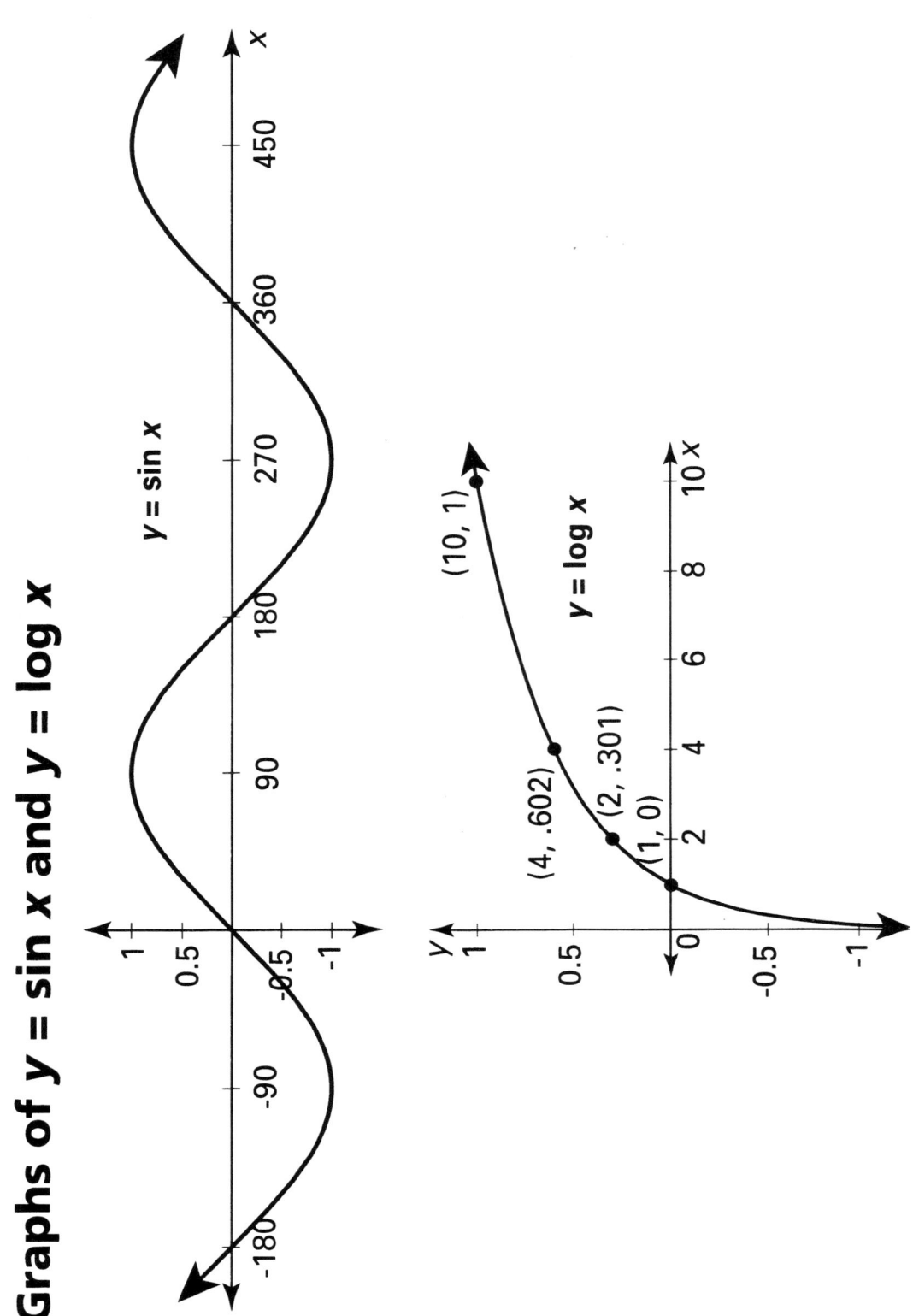